THE PILL
PROTECTION PLAN

CW00606493

THE PILL
PROTECTION PLAN

Gillian Martlew ND and Shelley Silver

GRAPEVINE

First published 1989

© Gillian Martlew and Shelley Silver

Illustrations by Gillian Martlew

British Library Cataloguing in Publication Data

Martlew, Gillian
The pill protection plan.
1. Oral contraceptives
I. Title   II. Silver, Shelley
613.9′432

ISBN 0-7225-1738-6

*Grapevine is an imprint of the Thorsons Publishing Group,
Wellingborough, Northamptonshire, NN8 2RQ, England*

Printed in Great Britain by Richard Clay Limited, Bungay, Suffolk

1 3 5 7 9 10 8 6 4 2

CONTENTS

DISCLAIMER

The medical and pharmaceutical information contained in this book has been compiled as a result of careful review of medical and scientific literature, and is provided only as educational information. It is not intended in any way as a substitute for the advice of a doctor, nor to be used in the place of medical care. The natural remedies and nutritional information found throughout this book are not intended as medical advice or to replace any information given to you by a doctor. No statement contained in this book shall be construed as a claim of cure or palliative for any condition of ill health. Every effort has been made to produce accurate information, but neither the authors nor the publishers accept any liability, however arising, from the use of any of the information contained herein, by any person whatsoever.

DEDICATION

To Gerry, David and Joan, Dr Jensen,
Dr Barbeau, and Jeanne Kellogg.

*For all knowledge and wonder (which is the seed of all
knowledge) is an impression of pleasure itself.*

Francis Bacon

PREFACE

About 150 million women worldwide use oral contraceptives, and, in the UK, the Pill may be used by up to 28 per cent of all sexually active women. The Pill is the most widely researched drug in the world. Since its approval by the US Food and Drug Administration in 1960, the high-risk groups for serious side-effects have been identified, and research has produced safer, lower-dose Pills which are as effective as their predecessors.

A reassuring statistic puts the estimated risk of suffering from a serious side-effect of the Pill at 50,000 to one, and the chance of dying as a result of it at 100,000 to one. However, like numerous drugs, the Pill may not be found to cause specific health problems until it has been used for a certain number of years, and with different sectors of the population. A serious side-effect may be relatively rare, and it may not be recognized, or equated as a side-effect of a specific drug until enough statistical data exists to prove, or establish a link between it and the drug in question.

Information and data on drugs takes years to build up, correlate and draw scientific conclusions about. So in five years, another serious side-effect may be linked with the Pill which is not obvious now. The Pill, like most drugs, is relatively young (it has its thirtieth birthday in 1989). Unfortunately it has already been proved that it takes time and an enormous number of 'guinea pigs' before all the possible effects become apparent.

New information about the Pill's advantages and disadvantages appears with such regularity that it can be difficult to keep up but, even with the avalanche of Pill data, many women still know very little about how oral contraceptives work, the possible problems and how the Pill interacts with other drugs — or how to protect present and future health while using this type of contraception.

The Pill is unique in that it is usually given for social rather than medical reasons, so this book's main objective is to provide a wide-angled view of oral contraception. This is the first consumer book about the Pill which includes medical facts coupled with non-drug, self-help advice. Like the highway code, *The Pill Protection Plan* can be used to interpret signs and signals, recognize problems, and steer safely around hazards.

Whether you have decided to take the Pill because it fits in with your lifestyle, or you are still weighing the pros and cons, reading *The Pill Protection Plan* is a positive step towards making the right personal contraceptive decisions, and towards making Pill use more pleasant — but, most importantly, it provides a plan which can be used to help optimize your present and future health.

ACKNOWLEDGEMENTS

Our grateful thanks go to all the women who shared their experiences of oral contraceptive use with us. Also to Valerie for proof-reading numerous drafts of the book and for her helpful suggestions. Additionally, thanks to Ann and David for their valued input. Our thanks, also, to Toni Belfield of the Family Planning Association for her much appreciated contribution to this book.

Chapter 1

ORIGINS

THERE WAS AN OLD WOMAN
WHO LIVED IN A SHOE,
SHE HAD SO MANY CHILDREN
SHE DIDN'T KNOW WHAT TO DO . . .

For thousands of years, people have been trying to find simple and effective methods of birth control and perhaps the oldest recorded form of contraception is 'withdrawal' or *coitus interruptus*. Throughout history, people have examined the botanical universe in search of plants with contraceptive qualities. In the first century AD, the Greek physician Dioscorides recorded a contraceptive drink called 'misy', in his herbal, *De Materia Medica*. Female contraception in ancient Egypt included spermicidal vaginal pessaries or suppositories compounded from ingredients such as crocodile dung and honey. It is thought that Arabian women used contraceptives made from mixtures of salt, alum and pomegranate pulp. Other vaginal methods of birth control included oxbile, elephant droppings, and even cabbage. However, ideas for preventing pregnancy were not limited to unpleasant sounding substances — some women dutifully swallowed tadpoles and others ate bees, while a more athletic approach was to jump up and down and sneeze after intercourse, a method purported to dislodge semen and prevent pregnancy.

Women always seem to have taken most of the responsibility for protecting themselves against pregnancy and, although the sheath has been used since the time of the Egyptians, it was not recorded as an effective contraceptive until the eighteenth century being rather to protect against venereal disease. Rubber vaginal pessaries appeared in the latter half of the nineteenth century and were dubbed the 'Dutch cap'. Around this time, contraceptive pessaries containing quinine sulphate were also available. But, in spite of the enthusiasm to find contraceptives, there was also a great deal of opposition to them, especially in the nineteenth and early twentieth centuries. In 1873, the Comstock Act which classified all contraceptive devices and literature as obscene was passed in the USA. Some doctors believed that contraception could lead to numerous diseases including cancer and nervous or mental disorders. However, none of this deterred the quest for pregnancy prevention, and this period also saw the beginnings of research which would lead to a better understanding of the reproductive system — and eventually to the Pill.

PIONEERS, RESEARCH, AND DISCOVERIES

Marie Stopes' controversial books on contraception and family planning, *Married Love* and *Wise Parenthood* were published in 1918. Three years later, she and her husband opened the first British birth control clinic to provide women with advice and simple forms of contraception. This angered many people, and a doctor called Halliday Sutherland sent out pamphlets which accused her of conducting harmful experiments on the poor and ignorant. Marie Stopes countered this by issuing a writ for libel against Sutherland, and the proceedings became more of a moral debate than a court case. Sutherland insisted that sex without pregnancy would lower the nation's morality, but, although he eventually won the case, it did not stop Marie Stopes' work, or the formation of other birth control societies.

During the 1920s, the role of the ovaries, pituitary gland and hormones in reproduction was researched. Dr Ludwig Haberland conducted experiments on mice, with extracts from the ovaries of pregnant animals. He found that these extracts could produce temporary sterility, and, for the first time, suggested that they might be used for contraception.

In 1930, the Minister of Health authorized local health authorities to give contraceptive advice to women in medical need, and, in 1936, there was a change in the inhibitory nineteenth century law which governed contraception — and in America, the Comstock Act was reinterpreted to allow doctors to prescribe contraceptives if they were considered essential to the health of the patient.

The 1930s also saw many scientific advances in the understanding of the reproductive system, and more was discovered about the role of the pituitary gland in controlling fertility. Oestrogen and progesterone were isolated and separated and used to conduct more precise experiments, but at this time the production of hormones was extremely expensive. The ovaries of literally thousands of animals were required to produce a few milligrams of usable hormone.

The expense and difficulty of extracting hormones from animal sources continued to plague research, but, in the late 1930s and early 1940s an American chemist, Russell Marker, synthesized progesterone less expensively from plant roots. Towards the end of the 1940s a number of different progestins had also been synthesized and, in 1950, Carl Djerassi and colleagues synthesized norethindrone, the first progesterone which could be administered orally without being destroyed by the digestive system.

THE PILL

Surprisingly, none of this research had been aimed specifically at producing an oral contraceptive and, although the idea had been suggested, the articles remained buried in medical literature. In the 1950s, the American birth control pioneer Margaret Sanger and her wealthy partner Mrs McCormack, encouraged and funded the work of reproductive biologist Gregory Pincus and gynaecologist John Rock, whose research culminated in the development of the Pill. In 1960, the Food and Drug Administration in America gave the go-ahead to Enovid, the first oral contraceptive. Conovid, Conovid E and Anovlar were later approved by the Family Planning Association of Great Britain and, in 1961, the first British Pill was marketed.

Since the Pill's introduction, it has gradually been refined, and there are now many variations available to enable doctors to choose the one most appropriate for each patient. The amount of hormones contained in oral contraceptives has been substantially reduced over the years, and research continues to make this and other methods of birth control safer and even easier to use.

Chapter 2

THE MENSTRUAL CYCLE SIMPLIFIED

In order to understand how the Pill prevents conception, it helps to understand how the menstrual cycle works.

The term 'menstrual cycle' is a catch-all for the different phases the
body goes through to prepare the lining of the womb for the implantation
and subsequent support of a fertilized egg (ovum) and which ends in
menstruation (a period) if no ovum is fertilized. This cycle, usually lasts
about a month, and is caused by a number of hormones which cause
several processes: the maturation and release of an ovum from the ovary,
the preparation of the womb lining (endometrium) to receive a fertile
ovum and the shedding of the endometrium if no ovum is fertilized.

The length of this cycle varies from woman to woman, and, in some
women, from month to month. Most cycles are 26–31 days long, but some
can be as long as 41 days, and others are much shorter than 26 days.
The cycle can be divided into three phases: the *menstrual* phase (days
1–5, menstruation occurs during this phase), the *pre-ovulatory* or *follicular*
phase (days 5–13, during which the ovary is prepared to release an ovum.
It is this phase that varies in length, determining the length of the cycle),
and the *secretory* phase (days 14–28 if the cycle is 28 days long.
Progesterone is secreted from the corpus luteum in the egg-releasing
ovum during this stage which stimulates menstruation). Ovulation occurs
around day 13 (later if the pre-ovulatory phase is prolonged).

The menstrual cycle is governed by two main hormones: oestrogen,
which is produced by the ovaries, and progesterone, produced mainly
by the adrenal glands, but also by the ovaries. These hormones are follicle-
stimulating hormone (FSH) and luteinizing hormone (LH). The creation
and release of these hormones are stimulated by the changing levels
of progesterone and oestrogen. FSH stimulates the growth of the follicles

(egg sacs) in the ovary, which, in turn, causes oestrogen and progesterone to be produced and an egg to be matured ready for fertilization. LH causes the follicle to burst and the mature egg to be released into the fallopian tube. This is called ovulation. LH also maintains the spent follicle when it becomes the corpus luteum (yellow body) which is formed when the follicle collapses, turns yellow and begins to produce progesterone as well as oestrogen.

Because this process is a cycle, the explanation which follows begins at the point where menstruation has occurred (because the ovum has not been fertilized). It will take you through the cycle in a simple way to enable you to understand it clearly. If you are unsure of any of the terms used, you can check the glossary at the back of the book for a detailed explanation.

1   If the ovum has not been fertilized by the end of the menstrual cycle, the levels of two hormones, oestrogen and progesterone, are 'switched off'. The sudden drop in these hormones stimulates the dispatch of RH — releasing hormone. RH is sent from the hypothalamus to the pituitary gland, and causes it to release the hormone FSH — follicle stimulating hormone.

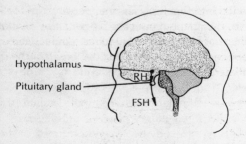

2   The FSH is carried in the bloodstream to one of the ovaries where it stimulates the growth of a number of egg sacs, known as *follicles*. Cells in the follicle walls produce oestrogen which is released into the blood stream.

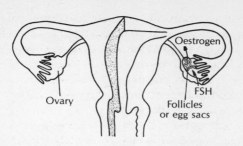

3 The increasing level of oestrogen in the bloodstream alerts the pituitary gland to decrease FSH production and by day 13 (if the cycle is 28 days long), results in the pituitary releasing a 'surge' of LH — luteinizing hormone.

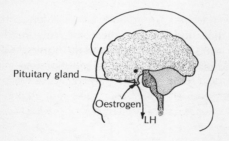

4 The LH is conveyed to the active ovary and causes the largest follicle to burst and release the mature ovum or egg. This is called ovulation and occurs around the fourteenth day of a 28-day cycle (or approximately 14 days before the next menstrual period if the cycle is longer or shorter than 28 days).

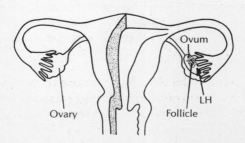

5 The released ovum is picked up by the fimbriae — 'sweeping fingers' located at the end of the fallopian tube. Contractions of the tube and the sweeping motion of tiny hairs, called cilia, carry the ovum towards the uterus.

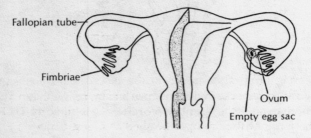

Fallopian tube

Fimbriae

Ovum

Empty egg sac

6 Once the ovum is released, the follicle, which is left in the ovary, collapses, turns yellow and becomes the corpus luteum (the yellow body). Oestrogen levels begin to fall off and the transformed follicle now produces and releases the hormone progesterone.

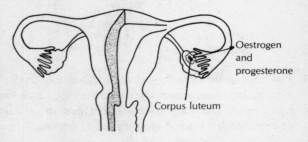

Oestrogen and progesterone

Corpus luteum

7 The progesterone manufactured by the corpus luteum causes the lining of the uterus to thicken and produce a nutritious lining in preparation for implantation of the fertilized ovum.

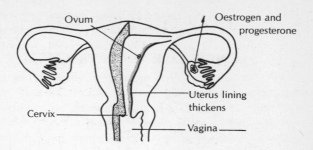

8 If no fertilization has occurred, the corpus luteum ceases to function and the production of the hormone progesterone is 'turned off'. This causes the lining of the uterus to be shed as menstruation.

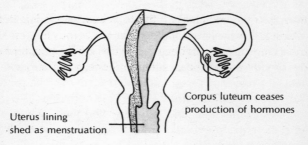

9 The 'shut down' of progesterone at the end of the cycle causes the hypothalamus at the base of the brain to send RH — releasing hormone — to the pituitary gland. This stimulates the production of FSH and the cycle begins again.

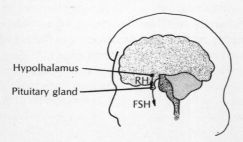

HOW THE PILL WORKS

COMBINED ORAL CONTRACEPTIVES

Combined oral contraceptives are statistically 98–99 per cent effective and are almost 100 per cent reversible; fertility is normally restored shortly after discontinuing them. They are composed of two hormones: oestrogen and progestogen (synthetic progesterone), which are comparable to, and produce similar effects to, the oestrogen and progesterone manufactured in a woman's body during each menstrual cycle. There are a number of different types of oestrogen and progestogen used in combined oral contraceptives and these are produced in varying combinations and different doses. The oestrogens and progestogens are absorbed from the intestine and metabolized by the liver and intestinal bacteria. Taking these hormones puts the body into a state of 'hormonal pregnancy' and this stops a real pregnancy from taking place.

In a real pregnancy, the developing embryo produces a hormone which prolongs the life of the corpus luteum. This ensures the production of sufficient oestrogen and progesterone to prevent the lining of the uterus (womb) being shed as menstrual flow. These hormones also inhibit the release of hypothalamic and pituitary hormones which stimulate ovulation. Absence of ovulation means that no ovum is released and so pregnancy cannot occur.

There are two different types of Pill available: the combined oral contraceptive (COC) which is a mixture of oestrogen and progestogen, and the progestogen-only Pill (POP). Combined oral contraceptives are the most commonly used because they tend to be a slightly more reliable form of contraception than the POP, and they are easier to use because they do not require such a high degree of accuracy in Pill taking.

The POP is only about one per cent less effective than the COC and is usually prescribed when a woman has an allergic reaction to the oestrogens in the combined Pill. The POP may also be prescribed for women over 35, especially for heavy smokers, as it seems to be less likely than the COC to increase the risk of cardiovascular disease in both cases.

So, by mimicking the hormonal status of pregnancy, the Pill prevents ovulation, therefore there is no ovum for sperm to fertilize. Progestogen also makes the mucus at the entrance of the cervix thicker and this acts as a barrier to sperm. The uterus becomes less receptive to fertilized ova so even if ovulation *does* occur and an ovum is fertilized, it won't implant in the uterus. In addition, it is thought that the movement of the ovum along the fallopian tube is slowed, which decreases the chance of sperm reaching it in time for fertilization.

THE MINI-PILL

Oral contraceptives which contain only progestogen are 96–98 per cent effective, and they are also an almost 100 per cent reversible method of birth control. Mini-Pills are produced from a number of different progestogens, in a variety of different doses. The progestogen contained in the mini-Pill is comparable to, and produces similar effects to, the progesterone produced in a woman's body during each menstrual cycle. Progestogens are absorbed through the intestines and metabolized chiefly in the liver and by intestinal bacteria. The main function of the mini-Pill is to cause the cervical mucus to thicken at the entrance of the womb. It also slows the movement of ova along the fallopian tubes and makes the lining of the womb less receptive to a fertilized egg, thus decreasing the chance of sperm reaching and fertilizing a mature ovum. Ovulation does occur in over 60 per cent of cycles in progestogen-only Pill use which can mean it is less effective than the combined Pill.

Chapter 3

Oral Contraceptive Fact Sheets

It is most likely that you are taking one of the many varieties of combined oral contraceptive, but if your doctor has prescribed the progestogen-only Pill for you, it is possible to identify it by noting the name on the packet and checking Fact Sheet Two to see if it is listed under the 'brand name' section. If it does not appear, you have been prescribed a combined oral contraceptive. If you are still unclear after checking the Fact Sheet, your pharmacist will be able to help you.

FACT SHEET ONE:
COMBINED ORAL CONTRACEPTIVES

USES

Combined oral contraceptives are mainly used for the prevention of pregnancy, but they are also sometimes prescribed for some menstrual problems, pre-menstrual syndrome (PMS), and spotting or bleeding between menstrual periods. Because of every woman's unique differences in metabolism and hormone levels, there is a great variety of Pill formulas available. Your doctor will want to prescribe a Pill for you which contains the most effective low dose of oestrogen and progestogen to prevent pregnancy.

GENERIC AND BRAND NAMES

The *generic* name of a drug is the main, or chemical name. It is usually the name of the main pharmaceutical ingredient of the drugs in a particular group. The *brand* name is the registered trade name that a pharmaceutical company gives to their particular drug formula. Please note that the information on this fact sheet applies to oral contraceptives generally and not specifically to any one brand-name oral contraceptive.

Levonorgestrel may carry a higher risk of cardiovascular disease.

Generic name	Brand name
Ethinyloestradiol and norethisterone acetate	Anovlar Minovlar Minovlar ED
Ethinyloestradiol and norethisterone	BiNovum Brevinor Neocon 1/35 Norimin Ovysmen Synphase Trinordiol TriNovum
Ethinyloestradiol and ethynodiol diacetate	Conova 30
Ethinyloestradiol and levonorgestrel	Eugynon 30 Logynon Logynon ED Microgynon 30 Ovran Ovran 30 Ovranette
Ethinyloestradiol and gestoden	Femodene Minulet
Ethinyloestradiol and desogestrel	Marvelon Mercilon
Ethinyloestradiol and lynoestrenol	Minilyn
Mestranol and norethisterone	Norinyl 1 Ortho-Novin 1 Ortho-Novin 50

FIRST STEPS — WHAT TO TELL YOUR DOCTOR

During any medical consultation, your input is important. Try to make sure that your doctor is given as much information as possible about your and your family's medical history, including that of other medication you are taking, especially non-prescription drugs. The checklist which follows can provide your doctor with important information which may be helpful when deciding which type of contraception is best for you. A number of the items in the checklist are not absolute contra-indications to taking the Pill, and, if they do apply to you, you may simply require closer doctor-patient monitoring.

CHECKLIST 1

Tick any of the following which apply to you	✔	Notes
Angina		
Allergy to steroid hormones		
Asthma		
Atherosclerosis		Also if in history of yourself or family
Blood coagulation disorders		
Breast-feeding		
Cancer of breast		Also if in history of your mother
Cancer of reproductive organs		Also if in history of your mother
Cholesterol disorders		
Contact-lens wearer		
Diabetes		Also if in history of yourself or family
Dubin-Johnson syndrome		
Epilepsy		

Tick any of the following which apply to you	✔	Notes
Ergotamine migraine drugs		
Eye disorders		
Fibroids or ovarian cysts		
Gall bladder disorders		This also includes gall stones
Given birth or miscarried		If over a month ago, do not tick
Hardening of the arteries		Also if in history of yourself or family
Headaches or migraines		
Heart disorders		Also if in history of yourself or family
Hepatitis		
Herpes		Any history of, during a pregnancy
High blood pressure		Any in history of yourself or family
Hydatiform mole		Recent
Irregular menstruation		
Liver disorders		Or history of jaundice during a pregnancy
Multiple sclerosis		
Over 35 years of age		
Porphyria		
Pregnancy		
Rotor syndrome		Any history of, during a pregnancy
Scanty menstruation		

Tick any of the following which apply to you	✔	Notes
Severe itching		Any history of, during a pregnancy
Sickle cell anaemia		Also if in history of yourself or family
Skin pigmentation		Any history of, during a pregnancy
Smoker		
Stroke		
Tetany		
Thrombosis		Also if in history of yourself or family
Toxaemia		Any history of, during a pregnancy
Vaginal bleeding		Abnormal
Varicose veins		
Water retention		
Worsening of deafness		Any history of, during a pregnancy

TAKING COMBINED ORAL CONTRACEPTIVES

There are a number of different ways to take oral contraceptives and your doctor will choose the method which fits best into your lifestyle. In this section the different methods are discussed in general terms only, and you may find that your doctor decides to change certain instructions. It is important that you follow those given to you by your doctor.

Fixed-dose Pill

The combined Pill is usually started on the first day of menstrual bleeding and then one pill is taken every day for 21 days, then they are discontinued and this is often referred to as the 'Pill-free' week. During this time, bleeding similar to menstruation will occur, although it is usually less heavy than a normal period. This loss of blood is due to the womb lining being shed. During this time the Pill is still protecting against pregnancy providing the pills have been taken correctly and the next batch of pills is started on time. It is recommended to try to take the Pill at the same time each day, perhaps before the evening meal. (Taking it just before going to bed can increase nausea when you first start taking the Pill.)

If the Pill is started on the first day of menstrual bleeding, protection from pregnancy is complete and no additional contraceptive precautions are necessary. If it is started on any other day, additional precautions are needed for seven days after beginning to take the Pill.

Phasic Pills

Phased formulations were introduced in order to mimic the hormonal fluctuations of the menstrual cycle more closely. This type of Pill achieves the same contraceptive effect as the fixed-dose Pill but the monthly dose of hormones is reduced still further. Phasic Pills contain two or three levels of progestogen which begin low and are increased two or three times during a 21-day course of Pills. Bi-phasic and tri-phasic Pills are begun on the first day of menstruation and give immediate protection against pregnancy. It is very important to take the pills in their correct order. They are taken for 21 days, followed by a Pill-free week (with the exception of Logynon ED, which has seven sugar pills).

Every-day combined Pill (ED)

This combined type is sometimes referred to as the ED Pill — shorthand for the every-day Pill. Seven of these pills are not active, being made from lactose (milk sugar). This enables them to be taken every day without having to remember the Pill-free week. Like the phasic Pills, it is essential to take these in their correct order.

SIDE-EFFECTS

Because of individual differences in metabolism, it is impossible to predict how any drug will affect a particular person. Sensitivity or reaction to oral contraceptives can vary greatly from person to person and can often be related to the dosage of hormones being given. It is very important to pay close attention to any changes you may notice either when starting to take the Pill, or during its course. It is just as important to report common side-effects as it is to report those which are infrequent or rare.

If you experience any of the listed side-effects, or any other unusual symptoms, you should consult your dispensing pharmacist or doctor immediately.

This list comprises side-effects which have been reported during the three decades that the Pill has been available. Most of the side-effects are extremely rare, especially with the newer lower-dose pills, and it is unlikely that you will experience those which are not common. A number of the common side-effects are similar to those experienced in the first three months of pregnancy and will often disappear within this time. By reporting all side-effects, you can help your doctor to make any necessary adjustments to your prescription.

Common side-effects
    Break-through bleeding
    Breast tenderness
    Change in weight (either up or down)
    Changes in menstrual flow
    Headaches
    Increased blood pressure (This usually returns to normal when
      the Pill is stopped.)
    Nausea
    Spotting or bleeding
    Water retention

Infrequent or rare side-effects
The lower-dose Pills which are now used, have further decreased the chance of experiencing any of these side-effects:

    Allergy to either hormone
    Appetite change
    Asthma
    Benign liver tumours

Blood clots
Change in insulin requirements*
Change in sex drive
Change in vaginal discharge
Changed glucose tolerance*
Dark patches on the skin
Depression
Difficulty conceiving after stopping the Pill
Dizziness
Fatigue
Gall bladder disorders*
Gum inflammation
Increased cholesterol levels*
Increased triglyceride levels*
Itching*
Leg cramps
Less wax in ears
Light sensitivity
Ovarian cysts
Raynaud's disease*
Scalp hair loss*
Thrombophlebitis*

* It is very unlikely that you will experience these disorders unless there is any history of this condition in yourself, or your family.

The Pill may actually give some protection against ovarian cysts and cancer in some women. The Pill also protects against cancer of the endometrium.

Warning
The Pill should be stopped immediately and your doctor informed if any of the following occur:

Any loss of vision or double vision
Blood in the urine
Breathlessness
Coughing up blood

Dizziness or excessive and heavy nose bleeds
Eyes or skin become yellow
Fainting, collapse or sudden weakness
Numbness or tingling
Part of the body becomes cold or blue
Pregnancy
Severe migraine, or any unusually severe headache
Severe or sudden pain in the side of the chest
Severe stomach pains or tenderness
Sudden temporary weakness or numbness of the arm, face or leg
Swelling in a leg or calf
Temporary loss of speech or speech difficulty

If you experience squeezing or heavy pressure in the chest, or these symptoms accompanied by pain in the shoulder, neck, arm and fingers of the left hand; nausea; sweating and shortness of breath, a doctor or hospital must be called immediately. These are symptoms of a heart attack and delay could be dangerous or even fatal.

PRECAUTIONS

Whilst taking oral contraceptives regular (six monthly) visits to the doctor are advised so that routine health checks can be made. Other factors to be taken into consideration are listed below.

Additional contraceptive measures

At times when other contraceptive measures are needed in addition to combined oral contraceptives, for example, if you have sickness and diarrhoea or have to stop taking the Pill temporarily before an operation, natural family planning methods are not recommended. This is because changes in hormone levels caused by the Pill make these methods inaccurate. For instance, progestogen is responsible for the temperature change in the second half of the menstrual cycle. The extra progestogen hormones contained in the Pill can make this method inaccurate for some time after stopping the Pill. Progestogen also alters the cervical mucus, so again, the extra hormones in the Pill can make this method inaccurate. The rhythm method also becomes unreliable because of the changes in the cycle brought about by the extra hormones.

Breast examination
Breast self-examination is important so that any changes noticed can be reported to your doctor. See chapter 4 for instructions.

Confined to bed
If a severe or prolonged injury or illness confines you to bed, you should not take oral contraceptives. It is important to discuss this with your doctor.

Diabetes and Pill use
If you use insulin, you may need to have your dosage adjusted while using oral contraceptives. It is recommended that you use the progestogen-only Pill if you are diabetic.

Laboratory tests
The results of laboratory tests, including those for glucose tolerance and blood clotting can be affected by the Pill, so you should tell the person in charge that you are using oral contraceptives.

Leg in plaster
If you have a leg in plaster you should not take the Pill. This should be discussed with your doctor.

Risk of pregnancy
There are some factors which can decrease the effectiveness of oral contraceptives. See Checklist 3.

Smoking
Smoking can increase the risk of a stroke, heart attack and blood clots, especially in women over 35 who take the Pill. Smoking 20 cigarettes a day triples the chance of suffering from a stroke.

Sunbathing
Avoid excessive exposure to sunlight and sunlamps while on oral contraceptives, as you may be more susceptible to sunburn, skin rashes or patchy pigmentation.

Surgery

Oestrogens in the Pill can increase the risk of thrombosis or blood clots and it is currently under discussion whether or not oral contraceptives should be taken before major surgery. It is important to discuss this with your doctor if you will be having an operation. This does not apply to minor surgery which only requires local anaesthetic, anaethesia of short duration, or to tooth extraction.

Vaginal infections

Oral contraceptives change vaginal acidity which may increase susceptibility to vaginal infections. If you are prone to vaginal infections, it may be wise to ask your doctor whether you should consider the protective value of using a condom during sexual intercourse. See the chapter on natural remedies for information on, and natural remedies for, candida.

INTERACTIONS WITH OTHER DRUGS

Taking oral contraceptives with other drugs can change the way they work. Some drug interactions can be harmful. The use of safer, lower-dose oral contraceptives may increase the risk of pregnancy if any of the medicines in section one are taken at the same time. This is because the older, higher-dose Pills had a greater margin of contraceptive safety due to their larger hormonal content.

Always check with your doctor or pharmacist before using any other medication. If you are taking any of the drugs in checklist 2, you should discuss this with a pharmacist or your doctor.

CHECKLIST 2

1 The following drugs may decrease the effectiveness of oral contraceptives:		
	✔	Drugs which decrease the effect of oral contraceptives can increase the chance of break-through bleeding, and,
Antibiotics		
Anticoagulants		
Anticonvulsants		

	✔	
Antihistamines		therefore, pregnancy. Only broad-spectrum antibiotics may decrease the Pill's effectiveness.
Anxiolytics		
Barbiturates		
Guar gum		
Laxatives		
Liquid paraffin		
NSAIs		
Tranquillizers		
2 Oral contraceptives can increase the effects of the following:		
	✔	
Bronchodilators		Increase in drug effects may lead to increased side-effects and could be dangerous in certain situations.
Hydantoin anticonvulsants		
Oral corticosteroids		
Some beta-blockers		
3 Oral contraceptives may decrease the effects of the following:		
	✔	
Anticoagulants		Any decrease in the effectiveness of drugs means that they may not be helping you as much as they should be. In some situations this could be dangerous. The side-effects of antidepressants may be increased when taken with oral contraceptives, even though their therapeutic effects may be decreased.
Anticonvulsants		
Antidepressants, tricyclic		
Antidiabetics		
Antihistamines		
Antihypertensives		
Anxiolytics		
Danazol		
Insulin		
Lipid lowering drugs		
Thyroid hormones		

4 Further reactions between the Pill and other drugs:		
	✔	
Ergotamine migraine drugs		If these drugs are taken with oral contraceptives, and especially by smokers, it can lead to an increase in migraine headaches.
Oral antidiabetics		May cause unpredictable fluctuations in blood sugar.

INTERACTIONS WITH VITAMINS, MINERALS, HERBS, FOODS AND BEVERAGES

Vitamins and minerals

Never take any supplements within four hours, before or after taking the Pill. Do not take vitamins A and K with oral contraceptives as this could be dangerous, and avoid doses of vitamin C over 200mg twice a day as higher doses can raise oestrogen levels. Supplements containing copper should not be used while taking the Pill. (For explanations and other important information on vitamins and minerals see chapter 6, Optimum Nutrition: The nutrition equation, part one.)

Herbs

Herbs such as sarsaparilla, elder, liquorice, *agnus castus* and ginseng can affect hormone levels in the body, and should be avoided unless taken under the supervision of a herbalist and your doctor. Feverfew was once used to bring on suppressed menstruation and therefore should be avoided while taking the Pill, or during pregnancy.

Foods and beverages

A diet high in foods which can contribute to excessive cholesterol levels should be avoided, especially when taking oral contraceptives. It is recommended to follow the general dietary suggestions outlined in chapter 7, Feeling Good: The nutrition equation, part two.

The Pill can lower the clearance of alcohol from the body, possibly because it decreases the effectiveness of the enzyme systems of the liver. Because of this, it is possible that, when using oral contraceptives, you may feel the effects of alcohol sooner than usual, especially if you are an infrequent drinker.

Caffeine may increase the time it takes for oral contraceptives to clear through the system, and this may increase the chance of experiencing side-effects, especially if one is an excessive caffeine user or particularly sensitive to caffeine. Beverages and foods which contain caffeine include: coffee, ordinary tea, matté tea, chocolate, colas, cocoa, some cold remedies and medicines, and guarana, which is one of the highest natural sources of caffeine.

CHECKLIST 3: PREGNANCY RISK

The following can increase the risk of pregnancy while taking combined oral contraceptives. If any of them apply to you, it is necessary to use additional methods of contraception. Contact your pharmacist for advice.

	✔	
Just started taking the Pill		Use additional methods of contraception for 14 days. Discuss this with your doctor.
Just changed to a lower-dose Pill	✔	Discuss the use of additional methods of contraception with your doctor, including how long to use them.
Taking other drugs: Antibiotics Anticoagulants Anticonvulsants Antihistamines Anxiolytics	✔	Discuss the use of additional methods of contraception with your doctor if you have been prescribed any of these drugs or are taking any non-prescription drugs. Only broad-

Barbiturates		spectrum antibiotics may increase the chance of break-through bleeding.
Guar gum		
Laxatives		
Liquid paraffin		
NSAIs		
Tranquillizers		
Vomiting or diarrhoea	✔	Contact your pharmacist or doctor for advice and discuss the use of additional contraceptive measures.
Break-through bleeding	✔	Contact your doctor for advice and discuss the use of additional contraceptive measures.
12 or more hours late taking your normal dose, or the seven day 'off' period has been extended	✔	Contact your pharmacist or doctor for advice and use additional contraceptive measures.

PROLONGED PILL USE

During long-term use there may be the rare possibility that blood pressure will gradually increase and gall stones or gall-bladder disorders and accelerated growth of uterine fibroid tumours may be made worse by using the Pill. Benign liver tumours are another rare long-term side-effect and if you feel a pain or an enlargement or mass under the right rib cage, or on the upper right side of the abdomen then you should contact your doctor immediately. If the combined Pill has been taken for eight years or more this could increase the possibility of the very rare risk of cervical or liver cancer. There is also a raised risk of breast cancer in women who have used the Pill for four years *before* their first full-term pregnancy. Regular smear tests and health check-ups are advised as a precautionary measure.

Discontinuing the Pill

Many women become fertile after stopping the Pill so it is necessary to use other forms of contraception immediately. Natural family planning methods will not be reliable until the menstrual cycle has returned to normal and the periods have become regular. Other methods of contraception should be discussed with a doctor. It is also quite common for the first natural period to be delayed for six weeks to six months after discontinuing combined oral contraceptives, and some women may experience a return of PMS symptoms.

It is usually *not* advisable to become pregnant for three months after stopping the Pill, to allow for good pre-conceptual care for both partners. This should be discussed with your doctor, and you can check chapter 9 for self-help groups. (See chapter 8 for more detailed information about discontinuing Pill use.)

FACT SHEET TWO:
PROGESTOGEN-ONLY PILL (The mini-Pill)

USES

The progestogen-only Pill is often referred to as the 'mini-Pill'. It is used mainly for contraception, especially for women over the age of 35, for those who are heavy smokers, and for women who want to use an oral contraceptive but cannot tolerate oestrogens. It can also be used by women who are breast-feeding as this Pill does not reduce or alter milk production. The mini-Pill may also be used in certain situations where an oestrogen-containing contraceptive is considered inappropriate. Approximately 2-3 per cent of oral contraceptive users take the progestogen-only Pill.

GENERIC AND BRAND NAMES

The *generic name* of a drug is the main, or chemical name. It is usually the name of the main pharmaceutical ingredient of the drugs in a particular group. The *brand name* is the registered trade name that a pharmaceutical company gives to their particular drug formula. The following are commonly prescribed progestogen-only oral contraceptives. Please note that all the information on this fact sheet applies to the mini-Pill generally, not specifically to any one brand-name oral contraceptive.

Levonorgestrel may carry a higher risk of cardiovascular disease.

Generic names	Brand names
Ethynodiol diacetate	Femulen
Norethisterone	Micronor, Noriday
Levonorgestrel	Microval, Norgeston
Norgestrel	Neogest

FIRST STEPS — WHAT TO TELL YOUR DOCTOR

During any medical consultation, your input is important. Try to make sure that your doctor is given as much information as possible about you and your family's medical history, including that of other medication you are taking, especially non-prescription drugs. The checklist which follows can provide your doctor with important information which may be helpful when deciding which type of contraception is best for you. A number of items in the checklist are not absolute contra-indications to taking the mini-Pill, and, although the list is similar to that of the combined Pill, there are actually fewer contra-indications with the mini-Pill. If any do apply, you may simply require closer doctor-patient monitoring.

CHECKLIST 4

Tick any of the following which apply to you	✔	Notes
Absent/irregular menstruation		
Allergy to steroid hormones		
Asthma		

Tick any of the following which apply to you	✔	Notes
Atherosclerosis		Also if in history of yourself or family
Blood coagulation disorders		
Blood haemoglobin disorders		
Breast-feeding		Unknown risk, possibly less than COCs
Cancer of breast		Also if in history of your mother
Cancer of reproductive organs		Also if in history of your mother
Cholesterol disorders		
Contact-lens wearer		
Depression		Also if in history of yourself or family
Diabetes/blood sugar disorders		Also if in history of yourself or family
Dubin-Johnson syndrome		
Ectopic pregnancy		History of
Epilepsy		
Ergotamine migraine drugs		
Eye disorders		
Fibroids or ovarian cysts		
Gall bladder disorders		Also includes gall stones
Given birth/miscarried		If over a month ago, do not tick
Hardening of the arteries		Also if in history of yourself or family
Headaches or migraines		

Heart disorders		Also if in history of yourself or family
Herpes		Any history of, during a pregnancy
High blood pressure		Also if in history of yourself or family
Kidney disease		
Liver disease or jaundice		Any history of, during a pregnancy
Multiple sclerosis		
Pregnancy		
Porphyria		
Recent hydatiform mole		
Rotor syndrome		Any history of, during a pregnancy
Severe itching		Any history of, during a pregnancy
Sickle cell anaemia		Also if in history of yourself or family
Skin pigmentation		Any history of, during a pregnancy
Stroke		Any in history of yourself or family
Tetany		
Thrombosis		Also if in history of yourself or family
Toxaemia		Any history of, during a pregnancy
Trophoblastic disease		
Vaginal bleeding		Abnormal or undiagnosed

Tick any of the following which apply to you	✔	Notes
Varicose veins		
Worsening of deafness		Any history of, during a pregnancy

TAKING THE MINI-PILL

The progestogen-only mini-Pill is usually started on the first day of menstruation and then taken regularly every day at the same time for as long as contraception is required. There is no Pill-free week with this type of Pill, so it is taken without a break even through the menstrual period. It is very important that the mini-Pill is taken at the same time every day. Ideally, this should be about four hours before going to bed, because progestogen-only Pills have their greatest contraceptive effect about four hours after being taken. Because of the high degree of accuracy needed when taking this type of oral contraception, it is important to use additional methods of contraception if a Pill is taken even three hours late. If the Pill is started on the first day of menstrual bleeding, no additional contraceptive precautions are needed. If it is started on any day other than the first, then you should use contraceptive precautions for seven days.

SIDE-EFFECTS

Because of individual differences in metabolism, it is impossible to predict how any drug will affect a particular person. Sensitivity or reaction to oral contraceptives can vary greatly from person to person and can often be related to the dosage of hormones being given. It is very important to pay close attention to any changes you may notice, either when starting, or during a course of treatment and it is just as important to report common side-effects as it is to report those which are infrequent or rare. If you experience any of the listed side-effects, or any other unusual symptoms, you should consult your dispensing pharmacist or doctor immediately.

Most of the Pill's side-effects are very rare and it is unlikely that you will experience those which are not common. The common side-effects will often decrease or disappear with time, but should be reported to your doctor, especially if there is no menstrual bleeding.

Common side-effects
- Absence of periods or irregularities
  Breakthrough menstrual bleeding
  Variations in menstrual cycle length

Infrequent or rare side-effects
  Acne
  Allergy to progestogens
  Appetite change
  Breast changes
  Change in libido or sex drive
  Depression
  Dizziness
  Ectopic pregnancy
  Fluid retention
  Headaches or migraines
  Increased blood pressure
  Increased facial hair
  Increased triglyceride and cholesterol levels
  Nausea
  Oily skin and other skin disorders
  Rash
  Vaginal dryness
  Vision changes
  Weight changes

Warning
The mini-Pill should be stopped immediately and your doctor informed if any of the following occur:

  Any loss of vision or double vision
  Blood in the urine or saliva
  Breathlessness
  Coughing up blood

Dizziness or nose bleeds
Eyes or skin become yellow
Fainting, collapse or sudden weakness
Numbness or tingling
Part of the body becomes cold or blue
Pregnancy
Severe migraine or any unusually severe headaches
Severe or sudden pain in the side of the chest
Severe stomach pains or tenderness
Sudden temporary weakness or numbness of the arm, face or leg
Swelling in a leg or calf
Temporary loss of speech or speech difficulty

If you experience squeezing or heavy pressure in the chest, or these symptoms are accompanied by pain in the shoulder, neck, arm and fingers of the left hand, nausea, sweating and shortness of breath, then a doctor or hospital must be called immediately. These are symptoms of a heart attack and delay could be dangerous or fatal.

PRECAUTIONS

Additional contraceptive measures

At times when other contraceptive measures are needed in addition to the mini-Pill, for example, if you have sickness and diarrhoea, or have to stop taking the Pill temporarily before an operation, the temperature, rhythm and cervical mucus methods are not recommended. Progestogen can alter the body temperature and cervical mucus, which can make the forms of natural contraception which rely on these, inaccurate. The menstrual cycle may be altered by changes in hormone levels and this can make the rhythm method inaccurate.

Breast examinations

Breast self-examination is important so that any changes noticed can be reported to your doctor. See chapter 4 for instructions.

Confined to bed

If a severe or prolonged injury or illness confines you to bed, you should not take oral contraceptives. This should be discussed with your doctor.

General health checks
Whilst taking oral contraceptives, six monthly visits to the doctor are advised so that routine health checks can be made.

Diabetes and the progestogen-only Pill
If you are using insulin then you may need to have your dosage adjusted while using oral contraceptives. Mini-Pills are recommended for diabetics.

Laboratory tests
The results of some laboratory tests may be affected by the Pill, so you should tell the person in charge that you are using progestogen-only oral contraceptives.

Risk of pregnancy
There are some factors which can decrease the effectiveness of oral contraceptives. See checklist 6.

Smoking
Smoking can increase the risk of a stroke, heart attack and blood clots, especially in women over 35.

Surgery
Progestogen-only oral contraceptives do not carry quite the same degree of risk of blood clots during surgery as the combined Pill, but it is just as important to contact your doctor six weeks in advance of any major surgery so that the Pill can be discontinued if necessary. This does not apply to minor surgery with short duration of anaesthesia, or to tooth extraction.

INTERACTIONS WITH OTHER DRUGS
Taking oral contraceptives with other drugs may change the way they work and some drug interactions could be dangerous. Some of the interactions in checklist 5 may only apply to combined oral contraceptives, but if you are taking any of the drugs in the checklist, or if you are in doubt as to whether any medication you are taking, including non-prescription drugs, could affect the reliability of your oral contraceptive, you should contact your pharmacist, GP, or local family planning clinic for advice.

CHECKLIST 5

1 The following drugs may decrease the effectiveness of oral contraceptives:		
	✓	
Antibiotics		Drugs which decrease the effect of oral contraceptives can increase the chance of break-through bleeding, and, therefore, pregnancy. Only broad-spectrum antibiotics may decrease the Pill's effectiveness.
Anticoagulants		
Anticonvulsants		
Antihistamines		
Anxiolytics		
Barbiturates		
Guar gum		
Laxatives		
Liquid paraffin		
NSAIs		
Tranquillizers		

2 Oral contraceptives can increase the effects of the following:		
	✓	
Bronchodilators		Increase in drug effects may lead to increased side-effects and could be dangerous in certain situations.
Hydantoin anticonvulsants		
Oral corticosteroids		
Some beta-blockers		

3 Oral contraceptives may decrease the effects of the following:		
	✓	
Anticoagulants		Any decrease in the effectiveness of drugs means that they may not be helping you as much as they should be. In some situations this
Anticonvulsants		
Antidepressants, tricyclic		
Antidiabetics		

Antihistamines		could be dangerous. The side-effects of antidepressants may be increased when taken with oral contraceptives, even though their therapeutic effects may be decreased.
Antihypertensives		
Anxiolytics		
Danazol		
Insulin		
Lipid lowering drugs		
Thyroid hormones		
4 Further reactions between the Pill and other drugs:		
	✔	
Ergotamine migraine drugs		If these drugs are taken with oral contraceptives, and especially by smokers, it can lead to an increase in migraine headaches.
Oral antidiabetics		May cause unpredictable fluctuations in blood sugar.

INTERACTIONS WITH VITAMINS, MINERALS, HERBS, FOODS AND BEVERAGES

Vitamins and minerals

No data has been found regarding the interactions between progestogen-only oral contraceptives and nutrients. What does seem clear from the available literature is that oestrogens, rather than progestogens, can decrease the body's nutritional status. Optimum nutrition is still important however, and for more information, see chapter 7, Feeling good: The nutrition equation, part two.

Herbs

Herbs such as sarsaparilla, elder, liquorice, *agnus castus* and ginseng can affect hormone levels in the body and should be avoided unless taken under the supervision of a herbalist and your doctor. Feverfew was once used to bring on suppressed menstruation and should therefore be avoided while taking the mini-Pill, or during pregnancy.

Foods and beverages
A diet high in foods which can contribute to excess cholesterol levels should be avoided, especially when taking combined or progestogen-only oral contraceptives. It is recommended that you follow the general dietary suggestions outlined in chapter 7, Feeling good: The nutrition equation, part two.

Combined oral contraceptives can lower the clearance of alcohol from the body, possibly by decreasing the effectiveness of liver enzyme systems. Because of this it is possible that while using oral contraceptives, you may feel the effects of alcohol sooner than usual, especially if you are an infrequent drinker. It is not clear from the research whether progestogen-only oral contraceptives also have this effect, but it is generally accepted that precautions for the combined Pill apply also to the mini-Pill.

Caffeine may double the time it takes for oral contraceptives to clear through the system, and this may increase the chance of experiencing side-effects. Beverages and foods which contain caffeine include: coffee, ordinary tea, matté tea, chocolate, colas, some cold remedies and medicines, and guarana, which is one of the richest natural sources of caffeine.

CHECKLIST 6: PREGNANCY RISK

The following can increase the risk of pregnancy while taking progestogen-only oral contraceptives. If any of them apply to you, it is necessary to use additional methods of contraception and contact your pharmacist for advice.

	✔	
Just started taking the Pill		Use additional methods of contraception for 14 days. Discuss this with your doctor.

	✔	
Just changed to a lower-dose Pill		Discuss the use of additional methods of contraception with your doctor, including how long to use them.
Taking other drugs:	✔	Discuss the use of additional methods of contraception with your doctor if you have been prescribed any of these drugs or are taking any non-prescription drugs. Only broad-spectrum antibiotics may increase the chance of break-through bleeding.
Antibiotics		
Anticoagulants		
Anticonvulsants		
Antihistamines		
Anxiolytics		
Barbiturates		
Guar gum		
Laxatives		
Liquid paraffin		
NSAIs		
Tranquillizers		
Vomiting or diarrhoea	✔	Contact your pharmacist or doctor for advice and discuss the use of additional contraceptive measures.
Break-through bleeding	✔	Contact your doctor for advice and discuss the use of additional contraceptive measures.
Three or more hours late taking your normal dose	✔	Contact your pharmacist or doctor for advice and use additional contraceptive measures.

PROLONGED MINI-PILL USE

During long-term use, there may be the rare possibility of gradual blood pressure increase. Regular health check-ups are advised and this should be discussed with your doctor or local family planning clinic.

Discontinuing the mini-Pill

The return of fertility after stopping the mini-Pill is usually faster than with the combined Pill, so it is necessary to use other forms of contraception immediately. The rhythm or mucus methods will not be reliable until the menstrual cycle has returned to normal and the periods have become regular. Other methods of contraception should be discussed with a doctor.

If you have stopped the Pill in order to conceive then it is important to discuss this with your doctor or family planning clinic before you try to become pregnant. This is because it may be necessary to wait a little while before conception, although this is less likely than after discontinuing combined oral contraceptives.

SIDE-EFFECTS QUICK REFERENCE CHART

If you are experiencing side-effects, use checklist 7 to find out which of the hormones in the Pill could be contributing to the problem. The chart also shows what your doctor's course of action may be when you report the side-effects. *Please note that this is only a guide. Your doctor will advise you according to your own individual needs.*

CHECKLIST 7

Side-effect	Hormone which may be mainly responsible	Your GP may suggest:
Acne	Progestogen	Oestrogen increase, progestogen decrease
Appetite increase	Either	Oestrogen decrease, progestogen decrease
Break-through bleeding	Progestogen	Oestrogen increase

Side-effect	Hormone which may be mainly responsible	Your GP may suggest:
Breast or uterus cancer	Either	Stop Pill
Breast size decreased	Progestogen	Oestrogen increase
Breast tenderness	Oestrogen	Mini-Pill
Cholesterol levels elevated	Either	Both hormones decreased or stopped
Contact lens discomfort	Oestrogen	Oestrogen decrease, or mini-Pill
Depression	Progestogen	Oestrogen increase, progestogen decrease
Fluid retention	Oestrogen	Oestrogen decrease, or mini-Pill
Gall bladder disorders	Either	Stop Pill
Hair thinning or loss	Progestogen	Oestrogen increase, progestogen decrease
Heart attack symptoms	Either	Stop Pill
Increased facial hair	Progestogen	Oestrogen increase, progestogen decrease
Increased fibroids	Either	Mini-Pill, or stop Pill
Increased light sensitivity	Oestrogen	Oestrogen decrease, or mini-Pill
Increased vaginal discharge	Oestrogen	Oestrogen decrease
Liver disease	Either	Stop Pill

Side-effect	Hormone which may be mainly responsible	Your GP may suggest:
Menstrual flow too heavy	Oestrogen	Oestrogen decrease, progestogen increase
Menstrual flow too light	Progestogen	Oestrogen increase
Nausea or vomiting	Oestrogen	Oestrogen decrease, or mini-Pill
Severe headache/ migraine	Either	Stop Pill
Sex-drive decreased	Progestogen	Oestrogen increase, progestogen decrease
Skin pigmentation	Oestrogen	Mini-Pill
Thrombophlebitis	Either	Stop Pill
Urinary tract infection	Oestrogen	Oestrogen decrease
Vaginal dryness	Progestogen	Oestrogen increase
Varicose veins	Oestrogen	Oestrogen decrease
Vision disorders	Either	Stop Pill
Weight gain	Either	Oestrogen and progestogen decreased
Yeast infections	Oestrogen	Oestrogen decrease

Chapter 4

Preventative
Self-Help

Before prescribing you the Pill, your doctor will give you a thorough examination, including the breasts and pelvic organs, and your blood pressure will be taken, if necessary. Health checks will be repeated at twice-yearly intervals and can help to decrease the risk of suffering from a number of health problems while taking oral contraceptives. There are also steps each woman can take to protect her own health, and the following suggestions outline some cautions and simple self-help techniques.

AIDS

The Pill offers from about 96–99 per cent protection from pregnancy but, unlike the condom, it does not offer any protection at all against AIDS — acquired immune deficiency syndrome. With the advent of new and potentially lethal viruses like AIDS, the Pill's ability to protect against pregnancy, but not against diseases which can be transmitted through sexual contact means that protective barrier methods of contraception, such as the condom, are necessary anyway. Paradoxically, this was one of the methods which the Pill was originally intended to replace. Research shows that the AIDS virus can be transmitted in a number of ways, although it must be passed into the bloodstream before it becomes a threat. The semen of a man infected with AIDS can carry this virus and if it enters another person's body through a cut, graze, open wound or split in the skin, they could be at risk of developing AIDS or becoming a carrier themselves.

If you or your partner have other sexual contacts outside your relationship, or if either of you have had any other relationships in the last several years then you should consider the importance of using a condom correctly every time you have sexual intercourse. When used carefully, a condom retains the semen emitted during sex and prevents it from entering your body. Apart from further protecting against pregnancy, a condom can be a barrier between you and AIDS.

See the section on self-help groups and associations if you would like to find out more about AIDS, venereal disease, and using condoms.

BREAST EXAMINATION

As a protective measure, it is advisable for all women to examine their breasts regularly. As well as self-examination, it is wise to visit a doctor for a check-up approximately every six to twelve months. During a self-examination it is important to watch for any lumps and to be aware of any physical changes in the breasts or nipples. This includes watching for any discharge from either nipple, and checking for changes in the shape of either breast, and changes on breast skin such as a rash, wrinkling or dimpling. If you do notice anything unusual, it is important to report these details to your doctor as soon as possible so that the reason for them can be determined and further action can be taken if necessary. Do not feel guilty about wasting your doctor's time if you do find anything unusual. Reporting it immediately could save time and worry later on. However, feeling a lump does not automatically mean that you have cancer — approximately nine out of ten breast lumps are benign or non-cancerous but they should never be ignored.

Breast lumps or sensitivity can arise during the use of combined oral contraceptives, although they generally reduce the incidence of benign breast disease, and, if either does occur, your doctor should examine you. It may be that you simply require an adjustment in the dosage of oestrogen contained in the Pill you are taking. Above all, whatever changes you notice, they should be reported to your doctor as soon as possible. A problem caught in the early stages is usually easier to treat than one found at a later stage.

HOW TO EXAMINE YOUR BREASTS

One of the most important aspects of self-examination is learning to recognize any physical changes that you see or feel. The following breast examination is best carried out on a monthly basis, approximately five days after menstruation has stopped. The examination only takes about five minutes to complete and can help you work with your doctor to protect your future health.

1 Begin your examination by becoming familiar with how each breast looks in a mirror in a good light. It is probable that they won't be identical, so become acquainted with what is normal for you.

2 Standing in front of a mirror with your arms beside you, look for any changes in the size of either breast or skin changes such as dimpling. Observe each nipple, noting any physical changes such as the nipple collapsing or turning inwards, or any discharge.

3 Raise both hands, clasp them behind your head and examine each breast again noting any changes in appearance such as lumps, swelling and drooping. While watching your nipples, drop your arms beside you and raise them into the clasped position behind your head again. Did your nipples both move the same distance?

4 Either lean forward with fingers clasped under your chin and elbows out, or place your hands on your hips and bring your shoulders forward. This should tighten your chest muscles and concave your chest a little. Once again check to see if you can observe any of the physical changes outlined in step 2.

5 Lie down on your back with your arms positioned at your side. Beginning with your left breast, position the palm of your right hand, with the fingers together and straight, on top of the breast, just above the nipple. Press very gently but firmly inwards under the armpit, feeling for lumps or anything unusual. Continue to go around the entire breast including underneath. Use the flat of your hand, not your fingertips. Work from the nipple outwards in circles including right up into your armpit.

6 Lift your left arm straight above your head and use the right hand to gently feel the armpit for any signs of tenderness or lumps.

7 Repeat steps 3-6 on the right breast, making sure that any changes, lumps, or discomfort are reported to your doctor.

DIETARY FACTORS

For general dietary advice and suggestions for breast health see chapter 5 on breast tenderness.

REGULAR CERVICAL SMEAR TESTS

The cervical smear test, or 'Pap smear' as it is sometimes called because it was pioneered by Dr George Papanicolaou, is used to identify pre-cancer of the cervix. This test involves the painless removal of cells by gently scraping the cervix with a sterile wooden or plastic spatula or cervical brush. The cells are then placed on a microscopic slide and sent to a laboratory, where they are stained with a special medium which makes the cells more visible for microscopic study. This test may also be of value in determining infections and other non-malignant changes.

Although the medical profession is still divided on whether or not the Pill can increase the risk of developing cervical cancer, most doctors agree that a cervical smear test should be done every three to five years, whether you are taking oral contraceptives or not. Your GP or family planning clinic will advise you on how often this is necessary. Your first smear should be taken within two years of first having intercourse.

INCREASING YOUR SAFETY MARGIN

Although there are a large number of side-effects reported with oral contraceptives, only a small number of them are commonly experienced. Keeping in close contact with your doctor is very important while using the Pill and every side-effect should be reported. You should feel comfortable enough with your GP to report side-effects, including emotional changes because, although many side-effects disappear within three months, some could be helped if adjustments were made to the type of Pill being taken. If you do not feel able to discuss side-effects of the Pill or other health worries, you may want to consider changing your GP. The Patient's Association protects and promotes the general interests of patients and they can be contacted for information on this by writing with a stamped, self-addressed envelope to the address under 'Patients' Interests' in chapter 9.

Remember that you do not have to go to your GP for family planning advice. You can go to any family planning clinic or hospital for this advice. You are also entitled to go to another GP if you feel you want to.

SELF-HELP ORGANIZATIONS

For a listing of other self-help organizations, how they can help, and how to reach them, see chapter 9.

Chapter 5

NATURAL SELF-HELP
AND HOME REMEDIES

Taking the Pill may lead to a number of side-effects which are not necessarily dangerous, but which can be annoying. Since the Pill works by mimicking the hormonal balance of pregnancy, some side-effects are similar to the problems experienced during the first three months of a real pregnancy. These can often be helped naturally, but the following remedies should only be tried with the advice of a doctor. This is important because your doctor can often help to decrease or relieve some side-effects simply by changing the Pill to one which seems to suit your individual body needs better. (See side-effects charts in chapter 3.) If you are told that your symptoms will subside with time and that a changed prescription is not necessary, natural remedies can be very helpful. There are usually several different remedies under each heading to enable you to find those which are most effective for your individual needs. You will also find a number of suggestions for vitamin and mineral supplementation, but a healthy diet should always come first. If you have obtained no relief within two weeks of trying a natural remedy, you should contact your doctor or a natural practitioner for more help.

ACNE

Acne can be an infrequent or rare side-effect of taking the Pill caused by the hormone progestogen. When reported to a doctor, a quite common course of action is to increase the dosage of oestrogen and decrease the progestogen, or change the type of progestogen.

SELF-HELP

Some of the progestogens used in the Pill can make some people's skin more greasy, and this may add to the chance of developing spots or acne.

Washing your skin thoroughly several times a day may help, but never use very hot water and avoid harsh soaps or cleansers as these can aggravate the condition. Choose a gentle natural cleanser and use plenty of warm water to thoroughly cleanse and rinse your skin. Try adding a splash of cider vinegar to the rinsing water as this can help to restore your skin's protective acid balance. Using fresh or bottled aloe vera juice on your skin after washing can help hasten healing and prevent scarring. Try to avoid the habit of frequently touching or rubbing your face with your hands as this is the main way of transferring grease and dirt to your face which can make spots worse.

Fresh air and exercise help to increase circulation and this carries away impurities and freshens your complexion. Using a 'slant-board' can be beneficial to your complexion, but it should never be attempted if you suffer from high blood pressure, a hernia, migraines, or if you are pregnant. The slant board should be used only under supervision if you have any heart disorder.

To make a slant board you will need a wooden board about three quarters of an inch thick, six feet long and approximately 18 inches wide. Cover the top of the board with dense foam padding and lay a cotton towel over it as an outer cover. To secure these, pull the towel tight around the board and attach it to the side or bottom of the board with drawing pins. Fix one end of the board **securely** about 17 or 24 inches above the floor; the other end should rest on the floor. When you are certain that the board is completely secure, you can lie on it with your head at the lower end and your feet above you. Relax on the board for about five minutes twice a day. Gently 'bicycling' with the legs is an optional way to increase circulation. This is best started slowly and gradually increased every day until you can comfortably include up to 30 of these exercises in your daily slantboard sessions. Lying on the slant board changes the body's centre of gravity and this can be very relaxing. It also increases circulation to the head and brain and helps the complexion. At the end of a session, rise slowly from the board by first placing your feet on the floor and slowly raising your body to a sitting position, before standing.

WARNING: Do not use the board unless it is completely secure. If it falls you could receive serious injury to your neck or back.

DIETARY GUIDELINES

Since progestogen may be responsible for acne, your doctor's probable dosage adjustment should help to clear up the problem. There are also some general dietary guidelines which may help. Try to reduce or avoid the following: alcohol, spicy foods, fried foods, refined carbohydrates and sugar. Eat more leafy vegetables and drink plenty of water every day. Make sure that your daily diet contains up to a teaspoon of cold pressed vegetable oil, such as a mixture of linseed, safflower or sunflower. Protein is important and can be obtained from foods such as fish, eggs, beans, grain and vegetable combinations, tofu, meat, dairy products, etc. Also include foods high in zinc, such as pumpkin seeds, wheat germ, liver, seafoods and eggs. For more information on zinc, see Optimum Nutrition — The nutrition equation, Part one.

Supplements for skin health include the B complex vitamins, and minerals such as zinc and GTF chromium. Chromium can help offset blood sugar problems which sometimes lead to spots. See The Optional Supplement Regime at the end of The nutrition equation, part two. Other supplements which may be helpful include acidophilus and evening primrose oil.

NATURAL PRACTITIONERS

For more individual help consult a homoeopath, naturopath or herbalist. To find a practitioner in your area contact the Institute for Complementary Medicine at the address given in chapter 9, Self-Help Groups.

ALLERGIES

The Pill can affect the body's immune system and cause an increase or modification in the white cells in the blood. This may lower the body's antigen-antibody response and therefore hayfever and related allergies may occur. When the immune response is low there is often a connection with the adrenal glands and this can also be related to certain types of allergy. If you are suffering from an increase in allergies or if your immune system appears to be affected (you are more susceptible to colds and infections, for example) you may find that a natural practitioner can help.

For more information you can write to the Institute for Complementary Medicine which is listed in chapter 9, and they can give you the details of a suitable practitioner in your area.

APPETITE INCREASE

This is an infrequent side-effect which can be due to either oestrogen or progestogen, and your doctor may decide to change your Pill to a lower dose type to counteract this effect.

SELF-HELP

Eating on the run and not taking the time to chew foods well can lead to over-consumption of foods because the appetite centre in the brain is notified too late that enough food has been eaten. If the hormones in the Pill do affect your appetite, it may be helpful to try to eat more slowly and chew food well. If you are not an expert with chopsticks then eating your meals with them can really slow you down!

The Women's Therapy Centre listed in chapter 9 holds workshops and group sessions dealing with eating problems.

DIETARY GUIDELINES

It may take a while for your appetite to stabilize, so dietary guidelines are also important. Try to eat whole, unprocessed foods and avoid 'empty calories' such as refined carbohydrates and sugars. Include plenty of fresh vegetables in your diet and substitute fresh fruit for sweets, biscuits and cakes, especially if you have a craving for sweet things. See chapter 7 for more dietary suggestions. Many women crave chocolate when their magnesium levels are disrupted (as they can be by the Pill) so it may be helpful to check that the diet contains enough of this mineral. Good sources include: brewer's yeast, soya beans, nuts, whole grains, seafoods and green leafy vegetables. For a more detailed summary of magnesium see the chapter on vitamins and minerals in *The Medicine Chest,* published by Thorsons (1988).

NATURAL PRACTITIONERS

For more individual help consult a homoeopath, naturopath or herbalist.

To find a practitioner in your area see: The Institute for Complementary Medicine in chapter 9.

BREAST TENDERNESS

Breast tenderness can be quite a common side-effect of oral contraceptives and is caused by oestrogens. Your doctor may decrease the level of oestrogen you are taking or recommend that you try the mini-Pill.

SELF-HELP

Please see chapter 4 for details on how to carry out breast self-examination to make sure there is nothing wrong.

DIETARY GUIDELINES

If your doctor has ruled out any medical reason for the breast tenderness, and the dosage of your oral contraceptive has been adjusted but your breasts remain tender, there are several dietary guidelines which may help this condition. Diet's link with breast disease, either as a preventative or causative factor, is a subject which has received much investigation. Oestrogen is known to cause fluid retention so it can be advantageous to keep your intake of salt and refined sugar as low as possible. It may also help some types of breast tenderness if nicotine, caffeine and alcohol intakes are kept to a minimum, or stopped completely. Caffeine sources include coffee, colas, chocolate, kukicha or banchu green tea, black tea, matté, cocoa, and guarana, which is one of nature's most concentrated sources of this substance.

Excessive dietary fat has been implicated in some breast disorders, so it is best to reduce saturated fat intake to a minimum. A diet lacking in vitamin F or fatty acids, may contribute to breast tenderness in some women. Vitamin F is found in cold-pressed vegetable oils such as olive, sunflower, safflower and linseed. A teaspoonful of virgin, cold-pressed olive oil included in the daily diet is the best source of vitamin F for breast tenderness. It is best to take oils uncooked and to avoid frying.

Evening primrose oil is helpful as it is involved in the manufacture of certain prostaglandins which, if deficient, may contribute to breast tenderness. If evening primrose oil seems to cause headaches, this can be remedied by taking the capsules during the day with food. For some people with temporal lobe epilepsy, large doses, over 2-3 capsules a day, have occasionally been observed to worsen the condition, and should therefore only be taken under supervision. Vitamin E supplements are often helpful and may be taken in doses of up to 400iu a day. However, unless taken under strict supervision, it should be avoided if you suffer from mitral stenosis, rheumatic heart disease, or are taking certain heart medications. If you are susceptible to high blood pressure then vitamin E can be taken in supplement form, but must be started at a very low dosage and gradually increased and, again, this is best done under supervision.

Recent research in Canada has shown that low iodine intake may increase the chance of suffering from fibrocystic disease of the breast. Iodine-rich foods include seafoods, sea vegetables, garlic, most vegetables and some wholegrains. If you are receiving treatment for thyroid disorders, do not try to increase your iodine intake without your doctor's consent as it may interfere with certain thyroid medications.

Sometimes breast tenderness is worsened by a high intake of two B complex vitamins, PABA and folic acid. These can increase oestrogen levels in the body, so PABA should be avoided in amounts over 30mg a day, and folic acid should be avoided over 200mcg a day. Very large doses of vitamin C seem to increase the bio-availability of oestrogen in the body and this has the effect of changing the Pill from a low to a high dose, and this can worsen breast tenderness. A number of herbs including sarsaparilla, elder, false unicorn, *agnus castus*, suma, ginseng and liquorice can influence the body's hormone levels and should be avoided when using the Pill, unless supervised by a herbalist and your doctor.

For more information about the interaction of vitamin E with prescription drugs see *The Medicine Chest*, published by Thorsons (1988).

NATURAL PRACTITIONERS

For more individual help consult a homoeopath, naturopath or herbalist. To find a practitioner in your area see: The Institute of Complementary Medicine in chapter 9, Self-Help Groups.

BRITTLE NAILS

Brittle nails can develop during Pill use, possibly due to oestrogen. It is unlikely that your doctor will consider it necessary to change your prescription if this occurs.

SELF-HELP

Brittle nails and white spots on the nails may be helped by supplemental zinc. Up to 30mg can be taken daily, and the diet should contain zinc-rich foods such as liver, pumpkin seeds, wheatgerm, and vegetables. For more food sources of zinc see chapter 6.

Evening primrose oil also helps brittle nails, as can protein, and sulphur-containing amino acids such as those found in egg yolks. For more information on evening primrose oil, see the section on breast tenderness in this chapter.

CARPAL TUNNEL SYNDROME

This disorder usually affects the hands and fingers, and in chronic or long-standing conditions, the shoulder may be involved. It is a disorder of gradual onset which usually affects pregnant women and those in their late 30s or 40s. Symptoms include tingling, numbness, and swelling, which occur when pressure is exerted on a nerve running through the carpal tunnel in the wrist. If it is found to be a direct result of Pill use, it is best to stop taking the Pill. If the condition is chronic there may be weakness or atrophy of muscles.

Although carpal tunnel syndrome is rarely listed as a side-effect of the Pill, it is known to be associated with combined Pill use. Vitamin B_6 deficiency is connected with this syndrome and B_6 requirements are increased by the oestrogen in the Pill. B_6 supplementation has been found to help if the disease has not progressed too far. Check that your intake of B_6 is adequate (see chapter 6, The nutrition equation, Part one). After consulting your doctor you may wish to take a 50mg vitamin B-complex tablet with your breakfast and 50mg of vitamin B_6 with your lunch for 4-8 weeks to see if it helps.

NATURAL PRACTITIONERS

For more individual help, consult a naturopath, homoeopath, acupuncturist or herbalist. To find a practitioner in your area contact the Institute for Complementary Medicine at the address listed in chapter 9.

CHOLESTEROL ELEVATED

Both oestrogen and progestogen in the Pill can cause an elevation in the body's cholesterol levels although this is quite rare, especially with the newer formulations of Pill. If this does occur, your doctor may either decrease the dose of both hormones or suggest that oral contraception is stopped.

SELF-HELP

Stress contributes to increased cholesterol levels in the body. Relaxation techniques, meditation, Tai Ch'i, and yoga, can all help you learn to control stress. To find groups or associations in your area contact the Institute for Complementary Medicine, details of which are given in chapter 9.

DIETARY GUIDELINES

Supplements of evening primrose oil, lecithin, and vitamin B_3 (niacin), all help to control or decrease excess cholesterol in the body. Please see the section on breast tenderness in this chapter for more information about evening primrose oil, and see *The Medicine Chest,* (Thorsons, 1988), for important information about vitamin B_3 and choline and inositol. For dietary guidelines check chapter 7.

NATURAL PRACTITIONERS

For more individual help, consult a homoeopath, naturopath or herbalist. To find a practitioner in your area see the Institute of Complementary Medicine, whose address is in chapter 9.

COLDS

At the onset of a cold many people's first instinct is to reach for the vitamin C. However, when using the Pill it is advisable to avoid taking more than 400mg of this vitamin a day. Larger doses can increase the availability of oestrogen and effectively change a low-dose Pill to a higher-dose Pill, resulting in a possible increase in oestrogen-related side-effects. Many people find that taking vitamin A at the onset of a cold works better than vitamin C, but again this is not recommended while taking the Pill. Combined oral contraceptives raise blood levels of vitamin A and supplemental doses of this nutrient could result in excessive serum vitamin A which could be detrimental. (See Oral contraceptives and vitamin A: Overdose symptoms [p81]).

SELF-HELP

The Pill can modify the body's immunity and, because of this, some women appear to be more vulnerable to colds and infections. At the onset of a cold, taking a teaspoon of Langdale's cinnamon essence in a cup of hot water three times a day after meals, helps the body fight infection. Zinc is one of the nutrients which is decreased by Pill use and this mineral is essential for the healthy function of the immune system. Zinc tablets or lozenges can be sucked to help sore throats and colds, but the dose should not exceed 15-30mg a day unless under supervision. If you prefer homoeopathic remedies, *Aconite* 6x may be taken at the first hint of a cold, or *Gelsemium* 6x helps if the symptoms are more advanced. Raw garlic is a home remedy for colds and sore throats, but if it does not endear you to your friends, you may prefer to use deodorized garlic supplements. Royal jelly can be used to help immune response and may help decrease susceptibility to infections in general.

DIETARY GUIDELINES

Try to reduce your intake of refined sugar, caffeine, black tea, and alcohol if you have a cold or, ideally, cut them out altogether. These can all deplete important nutrients which help your body's defence system to fight infection. Dairy products such as milk, eggs and cheese should be avoided for a few days to prevent excessive mucus production, especially if the cold is catarrhal or 'chesty'. Eat plenty of fresh or steamed vegetables and fresh fruit and drink plenty of fluids. The body will benefit if the digestive system is not over-taxed for a couple of days, so light foods and home-made vegetable broths are good dietary choices.

CYSTITIS

(See Urinary tract infections in this chapter.)

DEPRESSION

Depression is an infrequent or rare side-effect which appears to be due mainly to progestogens in the Pill. To help counteract this, your doctor may change your prescription to one with a lower dose of progestogen or a different type of progestogen.

SELF-HELP

Hormones in the Pill sometimes make women feel very emotional and this may heighten their reaction to problems. Talking to someone about your feelings often helps. Check chapter 9 for more information on associations and groups which offer advice and help for depression. Chronic yeast infections can occasionally result in depression. (See Yeast infections in this chapter for more information.)

DIETARY GUIDELINES

It is not often realized that nutrition plays a vital role in nervous and emotional disorders. Good nutrition combined with counselling can do much to restore self-confidence, and, in cases of transitory depression which seems to have no apparent emotional cause, certain supplements help, often within a few hours. Ensure that your diet contains adequate protein, but try to decrease or cut out altogether dietary items such as sugar, refined foods, coffee, and alcohol. These sometimes increase depression in susceptible people, and this may be linked with the fact that they increase the need for B-complex vitamins.

If your depression has worsened since you started taking the Pill, it may be due to oestrogen increasing copper levels in the body. High copper has been linked with depression, especially that caused by PMS and in women taking the Pill. It is thought to be caused by hormone activity increasing copper levels in the blood. It may help to discuss this with your doctor or a practitioner trained in the use of nutrients. For more information about copper see the chapter on vitamins and minerals in *The Medicine Chest* (Thorsons, 1988).

Transitory, mild depression may respond to vitamin B_6 supplements. A B-complex supplement can be taken with breakfast and 50mg of vitamin B_6 can be taken with lunch. Magnesium is commonly used by natural practitioners to help depression and can be taken, with calcium, in doses from 250mg to 300mg a day. Kelp is a rich source of many trace minerals, especially iodine, which is important for the normal function of the thyroid gland. Supplementary kelp may help in some cases of depression, but it should be avoided if your doctor is treating you for thyroid disorders. For more details on thyroid medicines see the chapter on the reproductive system and endocrine glands in *The Medicine Chest* (Thorsons, 1988). Zinc is very important to help the body excrete excess copper and it may be necessary to take supplements of up to 30mg a day.

NATURAL PRACTITIONERS

For more individual help consult a homoeopath, naturopath or herbalist. To find a practitioner in your area see: the Institute of Complementary Medicine in chapter 9.

GINGIVITIS

Symptoms of gingivitis include inflammation and redness of the gums accompanied by tenderness, puffiness, 'pink toothbrush' caused by bleeding, and bad breath or a bad taste in the mouth. It is thought that taking the Pill may make some women more vulnerable to this disorder. (Stress may also be a contributing factor.) Your dentist can help by removing plaque and tartar to discourage the growth of bacteria which attack the gums, and show you how to clean your teeth and gums properly.

SELF-HELP

The use of a soft toothbrush is often recommended, and it also helps to rinse the mouth with a herbal mouthwash (available from health food shops) after each brushing. Gum disorders can be one of the first signs of a vitamin C deficiency, and taking 200mg of vitamin C with bioflavonoids daily, at breakfast and lunch, frequently helps gum disease. Vitamin C should *not* be taken in doses over 400mg a day when using the Pill. For more information see *Colds* in this chapter.

HAIR THINNING OR LOSS

This side-effect is due to the progestogens in the Pill. Your doctor may decide to give you an oral contraceptive with a higher dose of oestrogen and lower progestogen.

SELF-HELP

Some women may lose hair due to the hormonal changes which occur during and after the menopause, especially when oestrogen levels decrease. In addition, it is quite common for hair loss to occur a few months after having a baby — hormones are often to blame for this problem.

HAIR HEALTH GUIDE

You can help keep your hair healthy by using a slant board once a day. (See the information in the section on acne in this chapter.) While lying on the slant board, gently massage the scalp, without rubbing it, then grip handfuls of hair, close to the roots, and tug them gently upwards. These exercises increase the amount of oxygen, blood and nutrients reaching the roots of the hair and, with time, can improve hair quality.

Avoid harsh shampoos, bleaches, perms and very frequent washing. As a general tonic, and to counteract the detergent effects of shampoos, massage either aloe vera juice or jojoba oil into the scalp, allow to dry, and leave overnight. They can be washed off when you shampoo in the morning. Also, try using a conditioner to reduce 'drag' when styling wet hair, and avoid using elastic bands or tight hair grips as they can damage or break hair.

Keep your scalp in good condition by rinsing your hair with water with about a tablespoon of cider vinegar in it. This helps to restore the pH balance of the scalp and can also help some types of dandruff, although it may make it a little worse the first couple of times.

DIETARY GUIDELINES

Elevated copper levels may be another contributory factor in hair loss and this can be offset by a diet which contains plenty of vitamin B_6, B-complex, and the minerals zinc and sulphur. Good sources of sulphur include garlic, onion, seafoods, beans, peas and lentils. Egg yolks are a source of two sulphur-containing amino acids: cysteine and methionine.

For sources of B-complex vitamins and zinc see chapter 6, Optimum nutrition — The nutrition equation, part one.

NATURAL PRACTITIONERS

For more individual help consult a homoeopath, naturopath or herbalist. To find a practitioner in your area contact the Institute for Complementary Medicine, whose address is in chapter 9.

HEADACHES OR MIGRAINE

If headaches or migraine become severe or more frequent while taking oral contraceptives, you should immediately contact your doctor for advice. **Do not try to treat them yourself, as a delay in reporting them could be dangerous.** *Do not use the herb feverfew for headaches while taking the Pill, as it could increase the chance of break-through bleeding and pregnancy.*

Mild, transient headaches can be helped by rubbing diluted oil of lavender into the temples, and under the nose where it can be inhaled. A neck and shoulder massage and a walk in the fresh air often helps to relieve tension headaches. If headaches occur in the Pill-free week you may find a change of brand helps.

LIGHT SENSITIVITY

Increased sensitivity of the skin to light can be caused by the oestrogen in the Pill. Your doctor may decrease the dose of oestrogen in your oral contraceptive or suggest that you switch to the mini-Pill which contains progestogens only.

SELF-HELP

While taking oral contraceptives, you may find that you tend to burn in the sun more easily than normal. It is best to try to avoid long exposure to strong sunlight, but, if this is difficult, use a good sunblock cream, with a sun protection factor (SPF) of 15 upwards, and wear a hat and light cotton clothing. There are many sun creams which contain the B-complex vitamin PABA (para aminobenzoic acid) and this can offer protection against sunburn.

If you are burned, the aftermath, if it is not too serious, can be soothed and healed with homoeopathic ointment for burns. Burn pain can also be helped by adding about four ounces of cider vinegar to a cool bath and soaking for about ten minutes. If you have an aloe vera plant or aloe vera gel, this can be applied frequently to help soothe the burn and heal the tissue. For more information see the chapter on natural remedies in *The Medicine Chest* (Thorsons, 1988).

NATURAL PRACTITIONERS

For more individual help consult a homoeopath, naturopath or herbalist. To find a practitioner in your area contact the Institute of Complementary Medicine, at the address given in chapter 9.

NAUSEA AND VOMITING

Nausea during the first months of Pill use is a common side-effect of the combined Pill and is due to oestrogen. Your doctor may suggest changing to a Pill with a lower oestrogen dose or, in severe cases, may change your prescription to the mini-Pill.

DIETARY GUIDELINES

Oestrogens can cause nausea, and decrease one of the most important nutrients used for its prevention: vitamin B_6. During the first trimester of pregnancy, many women suffer from morning sickness, caused by increased hormonal levels, and, because the Pill duplicates the hormonal balance of this period of pregnancy, nausea is a common side-effect. Vitamin B_6 supplements can often help this condition, along with the wholefood diet outlined in chapter 7. Up to 100mg of B_6 can be taken daily, ideally in a vitamin B-complex supplement at breakfast and as a 50mg dose at lunchtime. Vitamin B_2 in the B-complex supplement can colour the urine a bright yellow, which is a harmless reaction.

A fiery tea made by steeping a small slice of fresh ginger or a quarter of a teaspoon of powdered ginger, the ordinary baking variety, in a cup of boiling water is very effective against nausea. Allow to steep for about three minutes and sip slowly. Ginger capsules can be taken if the tea is found to be unpalatable. If you have a hiatus hernia then use this remedy only under supervision, as it can cause a burning sensation which may be painful. Another helpful remedy is homoeopathic Nux. Vom. 6x.

Avoid greasy and fried foods and try not to go too long without meals. Frequent small meals are often best, and snacks can include fruit, or pumpkin or sunflower seeds.

NATURAL PRACTITIONERS

For more individual help, consult an acupuncturist, homoeopath, herbalist or naturopath. To find a practitioner in your area contact the Institute of Complementary Medicine at the address listed in chapter 9.

PRE-MENSTRUAL SYNDROME (PMS)

Some women find that the Pill helps to decrease pre-menstrual syndrome (PMS), but it can occur during Pill use and after oral contraceptives have been discontinued. It is caused by the increase of hormones which occur at ovulation, and continues until menstruation. Your doctor may adjust your prescription to help decrease the symptoms.

SELF-HELP

The symptoms of PMS vary from person to person and include tension, bloating, headaches, anxiety, irritability, sugar cravings, aggression, depression, weepiness, lack of self-esteem, feelings of helplessness, insomnia, change in sex drive, skin eruptions, water retention, palpitations, back pain and cold symptoms. A number of these symptoms are recognized as oestrogen- or progestogen-related side-effects, and should be reported to your doctor before natural remedies are tried. To check oestrogen and progestogen side-effects, see checklist 6.

DIETARY GUIDELINES

If your doctor has ruled out any actual disease which could be causing your symptoms, you may find relief by altering your diet and perhaps taking some supplementary nutrients. Try to avoid sugar in all forms, including refined sugar, brown sugar, molasses, honey, maple syrup, and all artificial sweeteners. A little concentrated fruit juice is a good substitute. Both sugar and salt can contribute to water retention, weight gain, and depression, so they should both be avoided as far as possible.

Chocolate contains magnesium, so cravings for it may be due to eating a diet low in this mineral. Good magnesium sources include fresh fruit and vegetables, brewer's yeast, black grapes and raisins, fish and seafoods, and whole grains.

Caffeine slows down the clearance of oral contraceptives and can therefore lead to increased side-effects. It can contribute to increased irritability, and it also raises the body's requirements for B-complex vitamins. The Pill affects the enzyme systems in the liver which are involved in the metabolism of alcohol and, as a result, its effects may be more pronounced. Alcohol depletes magnesium, zinc and B-complex vitamins, and can alter blood-sugar levels, leading to fatigue, irritability and a number of other symptoms related to PMS.

PMS often causes a change in eating patterns due to blood-sugar fluctuations, and it often helps to eat small, frequent meals in order to keep blood-sugar more stable. Avoid large amounts of refined carbohydrates and heavy meals, but include snacks such as seeds, nuts and fruit. Base your diet on fresh vegetables and fruit, whole grains, beans, nuts, seeds, fish, yoghurt and low-fat dairy products. Include meat occasionally, unless you are a vegetarian.

A balanced diet supplies vital nutrients and, if supplements are necessary, they could include a 50mg vitamin B-complex taken either with breakfast or lunch, 200mg vitamin C and bioflavonoids with breakfast and 200mg with lunch. Vitamin E may be taken in doses from 100 to 400iu a day, but should be avoided if you have rheumatic heart disease, mitral valve prolapse (which is also called mitral stenosis), or if you are taking certain heart medicines. If you are susceptible to high blood pressure, vitamin E may be taken in supplement form, but must be started at a very low dosage and gradually increased. It is best taken under supervision. Kelp or a multiple mineral, and evening primrose oil can also be included. Supplements of histadine, an amino acid, should be avoided, as it can worsen some of the symptoms of PMS.

NATURAL PRACTITIONERS

For more individual help, consult an acupuncturist, homoeopath, herbalist, naturopath, chiropractor, or osteopath. To find a practitioner in your area contact the Institute for Complementary Medicine at the address listed in chapter 9.

URINARY TRACT INFECTIONS

Oestrogens in the Pill can increase susceptibility to urinary tract infections (often given the catchall name of cystitis), so your doctor may prescribe a Pill containing less oestrogen, and give you an antibiotic for the infection. It can also be due to having intercourse more often or with a number of partners.

SELF-HELP

Cystitis is one of the most commonly reported urinary tract infections and the main symptoms tend to be frequent urination which is very painful, accompanied by pain in the abdomen. If the cystitis is severe, there may be blood in the urine, back pain, alternating chills and fever, and general tiredness and aches. One of the main causes of this disorder is the transference of *Escherichia coli* bacteria from the anal area to the bladder via the urethra. This can happen during sexual intercourse, when inserting tampons, or after using the lavatory. Other causes include stress, shock, or using public swimming pools. Pressure on the bladder, caused by the womb or bladder being out of place means that urine collects in constricted areas and the resulting increase in bacteria may lead to pain and infection. Usually the body's immune system protects against infection, but when it is taxed due to poor diet or a stressful lifestyle, and if the vaginal pH is altered, cystitis or other urinary tract infections can develop. For most people, relaxation and stress control techniques combined with dietary measures will help to reduce the recurrence of infections, but these should only be tried when your doctor has ruled out any medical reasons for the disorder.

Wearing cotton underwear allows the skin to breathe and absorbs moisture, and this discourages infection. It is also important to keep your back warm. When washing the genital area, use a gentle pH balanced cleanser (such as a natural baby shampoo) and avoid perfumed soap which can be irritating. It is best to use sanitary towels rather than tampons during menstruation and avoid long, hot soaks in the bath. Exercise, fresh air, and good posture are all helpful.

DIETARY GUIDELINES

Sometimes prolonged use of the broad-spectrum antibiotics, which are often prescribed for urinary tract infections, may result in yeast infections such as thrush. This is because antibiotics can cause secondary infections by decreasing the population of important intestinal bacteria which keep yeast infections under control. If you suffer from recurring cystitis, you may have a yeast infection of the vagina, and this should be discussed with your docor. (See the section on yeast infections in this chapter.)

People prone to cystitis should avoid refined foods, sugar, salt, nicotine, coffee, tea, alcohol, chocolate and spices. Citrus fruit juices also aggravate the condition, but unsweetened cranberry or cherry juice is often beneficial. It is best to avoid chlorinated and carbonated water, but you should drink plenty of spring or filtered water during acute attacks of cystitis.

Herbal tea to help cystitis can be made from half a teaspoon each of buchu and *uva ursi*. Place the herbs in a teapot, pour boiling water over them and allow to steep for two or three minutes. A cup can be taken once or twice a day for up to a week. Alternatively, an infusion of shave grass tea can help. To make this, boil a cup of water in a saucepan, remove it from the heat and add a teaspoon of the herb. Allow to steep for half an hour and drink one cup a day for up to a week. Do not exceed the suggested quantities unless under the direction of a herbalist.

Supplements of vitamin C are important but should not exceed 200mg twice a day if the contraceptive Pill is being taken. Vitamin A is also very important and the diet should contain plenty of this nutrient although supplements should be avoided during Pill use. Significant dietary sources of vitamin A include dairy products, oily fish, liver, dark green and leafy vegetables and red, orange and yellow fruit and vegetables. Yeast-free vitamin B-complex and calcium and magnesium supplements can be an important part of a vitamin regime along with raw garlic or garlic capsules, and bee propolis. Both garlic and propolis have anti-infective qualities.

For more information on cystitis, and the vitamins and minerals mentioned in this section, see *The Medicine Chest* (Thorsons, 1988).

NATURAL PRACTITIONERS

For more individual help, consult a homoeopath, herbalist, naturopath, chiropractor or osteopath. To find a practitioner in your area contact the Institute for Complementary Medicine at the address listed in chapter 9.

YEAST INFECTIONS

Yeast infection is considered an infrequent side-effect of the combined Pill and was thought to be caused by the oestrogen in the Pill. This side-effect is less common with the newer low-dose oral contraceptives but, if it does occur, your doctor may decrease the oestrogen in your prescription.

SELF-HELP

Yeast infection is also known as candida, monilia, or thrush. It is caused by an overpopulation of *candida albicans,* a type of yeast which is related to moulds and fungi. Candida is always present in and on the body but is normally kept in check by the immune system and intestinal flora. Lifestyle, clothing, dietary habits, and the use of drugs such as broad-spectrum antibiotics, corticosteroids, and oral contraceptives can increase susceptibility to an overpopulation of yeast colonies and subsequently to yeast infection. Illnesses such as diabetes can also contribute to this type of infection.

As a side-effect of the Pill, candida overpopulation often manifests as vaginal yeast infection since oestrogens can cause conditions which encourage thrush or vaginitis. With the body's immune system or bacterial defences weakened, yeast colonies may multiply, colonize tissue, and emit toxins which circulate throughout the body. These toxins can lead to symptoms such as fatigue, intestinal bloating and discomfort, constipation, diarrhoea, irritable bowel syndrome, headaches, mood swings or depression, difficulty concentrating, irritability, nervousness, recurring cystitis, weight gain, food and chemical allergies and cravings for sugar, bread, and alcohol. If you are suffering from any of these symptoms then you should contact your doctor. He or she will be able to confirm whether the symptoms are caused by candida or another disorder such as a virus or intestinal parasites and advise on the best way of treating it. If you wish to seek the help of a practitioner familiar with the natural treatment of candida, contact the Institute for Complementary Medicine.

The immune system will have a better chance of controlling candida if excessive stress, late nights, environmental pollution or chemicals are avoided whenever possible. It can also help to take regular exercise in the fresh air and sunshine.

Yeast infection remedy

To help decrease vaginal itching, irritation and the unpleasant candida-induced discharge associated with yeast infection, wash the vaginal area once or twice a day with warm water to which a drop of tea-tree oil has been added. An effective and safe douche can also be made from natural ingredients. Yoghurt helps to restore the vaginal pH balance and feed healthy bacteria; raw honey has antibacterial properties, and aloe vera possesses both antifungal and antibacterial qualities.

Mix together:

1 ounce of plain live yoghurt
1 teaspoon of raw, uncooked honey
1 tablespoon of aloe vera gel or juice

This should be made daily and used once a day for up to a week, and then once a week for several weeks thereafter. Douche syringes and instructions on how to use them are available from chemists.

DIETARY GUIDELINES

Yeast infections can be greatly influenced, either positively or negatively, by diet. General dietary guidelines include avoiding foods such as sugar in any form, refined carbohydrates, strong or 'blue' cheese, yeast and yeast-risen bread, soya sauce, dried fruit, peanuts, mushrooms, smoked fish and meats, wines, beer and other alcohols. Try to eat plenty of whole, unprocessed foods and fresh vegetables, and 'live' yoghurt which feeds and encourages the growth of helpful bacteria. Include a little cold-pressed vegetable oil in your diet every day and also include plenty of protein. Although these guidelines are only general, they are quite restrictive so it is important to ensure that there is as much variety as possible within the allowed foods. It can also help to avoid eating the same foods more than every four days. For more information on diet see chapter 7.

The herbal tonic *Bio Strath* is produced from the yeast *candida utilis* and a common misconception is that this produces candida infection. This is untrue — *candida albicans* is a completely different strain of yeast. From various studies carried out with *Bio Strath*, it appears that its ability to strengthen the immune system may protect the body against *candida albicans* overgrowth, so it can be used to help prevent further recurrences when the candida infection has cleared.

Since the immune system is the body's main ally against yeast infection you can also help to support it with certain herbs and supplements:

● Raw garlic has antibacterial and antifungal qualities and can be used safely in the control of yeast infections. It also contains germanium, which is important for the immune system. If you prefer to avoid garlic odour, deodorized garlic capsules are an effective alternative.

● Oil of evening primrose is a useful supplement because its prostaglandin activity can help to strengthen the immune system.

● Acidophilus has antifungal properties and can help to restore the flora of the digestive tract.

● It is thought that people who are deficient in iodine may be more susceptible to yeast infection, and seafood and kelp supplements are a good source of this trace mineral. (Take under supervision only if you suffer from any thyroid disorder.)

● Selenium is another mineral which is essential for the function of phagocytes, white cells in the blood which help to fight infection. It is believed that people with a selenium deficiency may be more susceptible to yeast infection.

The B-complex vitamin biotin is used in the control of yeast infections as it is thought that candida flourishes when there is a biotin deficiency. It is recommended to take up to 300mcg of biotin daily. If you take separate supplemental doses of biotin it is important to take a yeast-free vitamin B-complex supplement once a day as well to prevent deficiencies of the other B-complex vitamins developing. Avoid taking B-complex after 4 pm as it may lead to sleeplessness. Vitamin B_2 found in B-complex can colour the urine a bright yellow, which is a harmless reaction.

NATURAL PRACTITIONERS

To help a severe case of *candida albicans* infection, or for more individual help consult a homoeopath, naturopath, herbalist or acupuncturist. To find a practitioner in your area contact the Institute for Complementary Medicine at the address in chapter 9.

Chapter 6

OPTIMUM NUTRITION
THE NUTRITION EQUATION
PART ONE

Optimum nutrition is extremely important when taking oral contraceptives. Quite a number of the Pill's side-effects can be related directly or indirectly to disturbances in hormone and nutrient levels. It seems that oestrogens, rather than progestogens, have the most pronounced effect on the availability of a number of vitamins and minerals and the way the body uses them.

Many of the B-complex vitamins are decreased, so are minerals such as zinc and manganese. The involvement of vitamin C is a little more complex — levels are decreased, but large supplemental doses have the effect of increasing the activity of oestrogen which can lead to an increase in side-effects, including further loss of essential nutrients. Vitamin E does not seem to be directly affected by oral contraceptives, but it may have a protective value against the rare risk of blood clots.

Levels of vitamin A, copper and iron may be raised, so, unless directed to do so by a doctor, supplements of these should not be taken while using the Pill. During Pill use, hormone withdrawal bleeds tend to be less heavy than normal menstruation. As a result, the monthly loss of iron may be reduced in approximately 60-80 per cent of women using oral contraceptives. Some estimates suggest that Pill use may lower the amount of menstrual blood iron loss by a quarter to half that of non-Pill users. Raised copper levels reduce minerals such as zinc and manganese and contribute to the rare risk of blood clots. It is important to avoid cooking with copper utensils and eating a diet high in refined foods, as these are often low in minerals and vitamins which are important to offset excess copper.

This chapter has been divided into two sections, Part 1 deals separately, and in detail, with the vitamins and minerals affected by combined oral contraceptives and gives significant food sources and other important data. Part 2 (in chapter 7) shows the importance of a healthy diet, helps

CHECKLIST 8: NUTRIENTS AND THE PILL

A	B₂	B₃	B₁₂	Bio-tin	Folic acid	Chol-ine	C	P	Cal-cium	Mang-anese	Cop-per	Iron	Zinc
▲ (increased blood levels)									▲ (increased due to raised absorption)	▲ (increased blood levels)		△ (increased due to decreased excretion)	
	▽	▽	▼	▽	▽	▽	▽	▽		▽			▽

Legend:

▽ (open)	Decreased due to more rapid excretion
▼ (solid)	Decreased due to lowered absorption
▽ (hatched)	Decreased due to raised requirement
△ (open)	Increased due to decreased excretion
▲ (solid)	Increased due to raised absorption
▲ (hatched)	Increased blood levels

with diet planning and gives sample menus, while 'boiling down' the information to present a recipe for health. At the end of chapter 7 a chart is included for an optional supplement regime including what to take and when to take it. If you wish to consider using any food supplements please check with your doctor first.

ORAL CONTRACEPTIVES AND VITAMIN A

Taking oral contraceptives can deplete the liver's supply of vitamin A, but blood levels of this nutrient are raised. This means that while using the Pill, vitamin A supplements, including cod liver oil, should *never* be taken, as this could lead to vitamin A toxicity. However, the body's ability to absorb vitamin A from food is *decreased,* so it is important to make sure that plenty of foods rich in this nutrient are included in the diet.

VITAMIN A FACT-FILE

There are two types of Vitamin A: pro-formed and pre-formed. Pro-formed vitamin A, known as carotene, is found in yellow, orange and green vegetables and fruit, and is converted to vitamin A by the liver. It is destroyed by heat and oxygen, and is lost into cooking water. The second type, pre-formed vitamin A, is found in foods of animal origin. It is fat soluble and can be destroyed by light, oxygen, and cooking in iron or copper pans. Pre-formed vitamin A is found in the tissues of animals and fish, and can be absorbed in the digestive tract in the presence of fats and minerals. The liver is the site of vitamin A storage. Nutrients which work together synergistically with vitamin A include, B-complex, vitamins C and E, inositol, zinc, selenium and manganese.

FOOD SOURCE GUIDE

These foods are listed in approximate descending order, but nutrient levels, especially of fruit and vegetables, can vary. Where the foods are grown, and the way they are grown, handled, stored and prepared determines their actual nutrient content.

Pre-formed vitamin A
Fish liver oils
Liver
Oily fish
Butter
Egg yolks
Cheese
Whole milk
Whole milk products
Yoghurt

Pro-vitamin A (Carotene)
All dark green vegetables, and yellow and orange fruit and vegetables contain a certain amount of carotene but some of the higher sources are listed below.
Carrots
Parsley
Spinach
Spring greens and kale
Sweet potatoes
Watercress
Pumpkin
Apricots
Watermelon
Mangoes
Papaya
Tomatoes

FACTORS WHICH MAY RAISE REQUIREMENTS

Alcohol
Antacids
Aspirin
Excessively high protein intake
Exposure to air pollution
Exposure to ultra violet light
Fever

Gout drugs
Infection
Lipid-reducing drugs
Liquid paraffin
Smoking

DEFICIENCY SYMPTOMS

Cloudy vision
Conjunctivitis
Dry eyes
Excessive mucus
Inflamed eyelids
Itching or burning eyes
Poor night vision
Poor quality finger- and toe-nails
Red eye rims
Skin or scalp disorders

OVERDOSE

Vitamin A supplements or cod-liver oil should *never* be taken with oral contraceptives, as the risk of vitamin A toxicity is increased.

Overdose symptoms
Blurred vision
Brittle nails
Diarrhoea
Dry, scaly lips, skin or scalp
Enlargement of the liver and spleen
Hair loss
Headaches
Nausea
Skin rash
Vomiting
Weight loss

If extremely large amounts of carotene are ingested, in the form of carrot juice or beta-carotene supplements, then occasionally the palms of the hands or the soles of the feet can turn a yellow-orange colour. If this happens, the source of carotene should be stopped or reduced until the colour disappears. However, if this problem occurs from an average daily intake of fruit and vegetables then it is important to ask your doctor to check your liver and gall-bladder function.

ORAL CONTRACEPTIVES AND VITAMIN B_2

The oestrogen in oral contraceptives may increase the body's need for B_2, possibly by stimulating reactions in the body which require it. Therefore if a balanced diet is not eaten, or if B_2 is decreased by other factors (see: *Factors which may raise requirements* in this section) it may be necessary to supplement up to 50mg of B_2 a day. As with all B vitamins, B_2 should be taken as part of the B-complex in order to prevent the symptoms of other B group deficiencies occuring.

VITAMIN B_2 FACT-FILE

Vitamin B_2, also known as riboflavin, is a water- and alcohol-soluble vitamin which is absorbed through the walls of the small intestine. It can be found in the kidneys and liver, but is not stored by the body. B_2 is often used as a food colouring because of its bright yellow colour, and, when it is taken in supplement form, it often colours the urine yellow, which is a harmless reaction. Cooking is not destructive to B_2 unless alkalis such as baking soda are present, but it is lost into cooking water and destroyed by the ultraviolet rays in sunlight and by fluorescent lighting. Other nutrients which work synergistically with vitamin B_2 include B-complex, vitamin C, manganese, phosphorus, and zinc.

FOOD SOURCE GUIDE

The foods are listed in approximate descending order but nutrient levels, especially of fruit and vegetables, can vary. Where the foods are grown, and the way they are grown, handled, stored and prepared determines their actual nutrient content.

Brewer's yeast and yeast extract
Liver
Wheatgerm
Eggs
Wheatbran
Meat
Soya flour
Yoghurt
Cheese
Whole milk
Green and leafy vegetables
Nuts, seeds and pulses

FACTORS WHICH MAY INCREASE REQUIREMENTS

Alcohol
Antacids
Antibiotics
Antidepressants
Breast-feeding
Fever
Oestrogens
Pregnancy
Smoking

DEFICIENCY SYMPTOMS

Blurred vision
Burning sensations under the eyelids
Cataract formation
Changes in the cornea
Cracks around corners of the mouth
Decreased energy
Depression
Difficulty sleeping
Dizziness
Eye fatigue and bloodshot eyes
Glossy and inflamed tongue

Gritty sensations under the eyelids
Headaches
Oily skin
Scaling skin on the face and head
Sensitivity of eyes to light
Trembling

OVERDOSE

If an excessive amount of vitamin B_2 is taken in supplement form, symptoms such as itching or burning may occur, but will disappear when the dose is reduced or withdrawn. Taking large quantities of B_2 without the other B-complex vitamins can unbalance them and lead to disorders caused by their deficiencies. Excessively large intakes of B_2 may affect the liver.

ORAL CONTRACEPTIVES AND VITAMIN B_6

The need for vitamin B_6 is increased while taking oral contraceptives possibly because oestrogen can stimulate reactions in the body which require B_6. If this vitamin is depleted, the body's metabolism of the amino acid tryptophane is decreased and, as a result, synthesis of vitamin B_3 is affected. B_6 is important for glucose tolerance and it is also involved in the production of a brain chemical called serotonin which is thought to elevate mood. This is why B_6 is often given to help depression, sleep disturbances and even headaches. If a balanced diet is not eaten or if B_6 is decreased by other factors (see: *Factors which may increase requirements* in this section), it may be necessary to supplement up to 50mg of B_6 a day. As with all B vitamins, B_6 should be taken as part of the B-complex in order to prevent the symptoms of other B group deficiencies occuring.

VITAMIN B_6 FACT-FILE

B_6, also known as pyridoxine, is a water- and alcohol-soluble vitamin crucial to many body processes. It is not stored in the body and is excreted in the urine. Heat, sunlight, air or freezing can decrease B_6 in food and some is lost into cooking water. Other nutrients which work synergistically with vitamin B_6 include other B-complex vitamins, vitamin C, magnesium, potassium, manganese and zinc.

FOOD SOURCE GUIDE

The foods are listed in approximate descending order but nutrient levels, especially of fruit and vegetables, can vary. Where the foods are grown, and the way they are grown, handled, stored and prepared determines their actual nutrient content.

Brewer's yeast and yeast extract
Rice and wheat bran
Wheatgerm
Whole grains
Molasses
Mackerel and fatty fish
Soya flour
Meat
Bananas
Brazil nuts
Salmon and other fish
Green leafy vegetables
Root vegetables
Pulses

FACTORS WHICH MAY RAISE REQUIREMENTS

Alcohol
Antacids
Breast-feeding
Dieting and fasting
Diuretics
Excessive, continuous intake of choline
Excessive intake of protein

Hydralazine antihypertensives
Isoniazid ant tuberculosis drugs
Oestrogens
Pregnancy
Severe vomiting during early pregnancy
Smoking
Some antibiotics
Strenuous activity
Stress

DEFICIENCY SYMPTOMS

Appetite loss
Breast tenderness
Decreased concentration
Depression or irritability
Dermatitis around mouth, eyes or nose
Headaches
Memory loss
Menstrual disorders
Nausea and vomiting
Nervousness
Sore tongue
Split lips
Tiredness
Weakness

OVERDOSE

There is usually no toxicity with doses of B_6 up to 100mg a day but this intake may cause night restlessness and vivid dream recall in some people. Excessively large intakes of vitamin B_6 over a period of time may cause reversible disorders of the nervous system, and liver damage. But, taken correctly, under professional supervision, B_6 is not likely to cause side-effects.

ORAL CONTRACEPTIVES AND VITAMIN B$_{12}$

Oestrogens in the Pill can reduce B$_{12}$ absorption and some vegans or vegetarians may be particularly at risk of a B$_{12}$ deficiency while using oral contraceptives. If the diet does not contain meat, milk or fermented soya products, or if other factors occur which decrease B$_{12}$ (see: *Factors which may increase requirements*), it may be necessary to supplement up to 100mcg of B$_{12}$ daily. As with all B vitamins, B$_{12}$ should be taken as part of the B-complex in order to prevent the symptoms of other B group deficiencies occuring.

VITAMIN B$_{12}$ FACT FILE

B$_{12}$ is a water- and alcohol-soluble vitamin also known as cyano-cobalamin as it contains the mineral cobalt. It is unstable if cooked with acids or alkalis such as vinegar or baking soda. B$_{12}$ is needed by every cell in the body, especially red blood cells, muscle, nerve, and gastro-intestinal cells. It is not easily absorbed from food and requires calcium and a substance called intrinsic factor, which must be present in the digestive juices, for its assimilation. Some B$_{12}$ can be manufactured in small amounts in the body and it is stored in the liver. Other nutrients which work synergistically with vitamin B$_{12}$ include vitamin B-complex, vitamins A, C and E, potassium, manganese, sodium and zinc.

FOOD SOURCE GUIDE

The foods are listed in approximate descending order but nutrient levels, especially of fruit and vegetables, can vary. Where the foods are grown, and the way they are grown, handled, stored and prepared determines their actual nutrient content.

Offal, especially liver
Sardines and other seafood
Eggs
Spirulina plant plankton
Kelp

Fermented foods such as yoghurt, miso and tempeh
Cheeses

FACTORS WHICH MAY RAISE REQUIREMENTS

Alcohol
Antacids
Some antibiotics
Anticonvulsants
Some antiParkinsonian drugs
Anxiolytics or sleeping tablets
Aspirin
Consistent and high intake of comfrey
Digestive disorders
Intestinal parasites
Oestrogens
Pregnancy
Smoking
Urinary tract anti-infectives
Vitamin C supplementation over 750mg daily

Note: A deficiency of B_{12} can go undetected for some time. Damage to the nervous system and spinal cord may occur during this time and pernicious anaemia may develop.

DEFICIENCY SYMPTOMS

Depression or irritability
Inflammation of the tongue or mouth
Loss of short term memory
Menstrual disorders
Mental sluggishness
Mood swings
Numbness or tingling in the extremities
Pernicious anaemia
Sore tongue
Tiredness
Tremors

OVERDOSE

Toxicity from B_{12} overdose is extremely rare, but a very high supplementary intake of B_{12} may mask the signs of pernicious anaemia. Taking large quantities of B_{12} without the other B-complex vitamins can unbalance them and lead to disorders caused by their deficiencies.

ORAL CONTRACEPTIVES AND FOLIC ACID

Folic acid levels may be decreased when taking oral contraceptives, possibly because of the stimulation of reactions in the body which require it, and because its absorption may be affected. If a balanced diet is not eaten or if folic acid is decreased by other factors (see: *Factors which may increase requirements* in this section), it may be necessary to supplement up to 1000mcg a day. As with all B vitamins, folic acid should be taken as part of the B-complex in order to prevent the symptoms of other B group deficiencies occuring.

FOLIC ACID FACT-FILE

Folic acid is a water-soluble vitamin which takes its name from 'foliage', as it was first found in dark green, leafy vegetables. It is destroyed by high temperatures, cooking with acids such as vinegar and is decreased when stored for long periods at room temperature or when exposed to light. A large percentage of this vitamin is lost into cooking water. Folic acid is not produced by the body, but the liver converts it to folinic acid and can store it. Other nutrients which work synergistically with folic acid include other B-complex vitamins, especially biotin, B_{12}, PABA and B_5, vitamin C, manganese and zinc.

FOOD SOURCE GUIDE

The foods are listed in approximate descending order but nutrient levels, especially of fruit and vegetables, can vary. Where the foods are grown, and the way they are grown, handled, stored and prepared determines their actual nutrient content.

Brewer's yeast
Wheatgerm and bran

Green leafy vegetables
Liver and organ meats
Nuts
Oranges or fresh juice
Beans and peas
Eggs
Brown rice
Cheese
Avocado
Meat and fish

FACTORS WHICH MAY RAISE REQUIREMENTS

Alcohol
Aspirin
Dieting
Illness
Injury
Isoniazid anti-tuberculosis drugs
Oral contraceptives and oestrogens
Phenytoin*
Pregnancy and lactation
Primidone anticonvulsants
Pyrimethamine*
Stress
Sulphonamides*
Trimethoprim anti-infectives*
Trimterene and other diuretics

* Supplemental folic acid can decrease the effectiveness of these drugs and should be taken with them only under supervision.

DEFICIENCY SYMPTOMS

Digestive disorders
Forgetfulness
Insomnia
Irritability

Megaloblastic anaemia
Smooth, sore or inflamed tongue
Tiredness
Weakness

OVERDOSE

An excessive intake of 15 000mcg or 15mg of folic acid per day can cause nausea, wind, irritability and loss of appetite in susceptible people. Long-term high doses can decrease vitamin B_{12} and may mask the symptoms of a B_{12} deficiency which can lead to pernicious anaemia and nerve degeneration if not corrected. Taking large quantities of folic acid without the other B-complex vitamins can unbalance them and lead to disorders caused by their deficiencies.

ORAL CONTRACEPTIVES AND BIOTIN

Biotin can be decreased by oral contraceptive use and therefore, if a balanced diet is not eaten or if other factors occur which decrease biotin (see: *Factors which may raise requirements* in this section), it may be necessary to supplement up to 100mcg a day.

BIOTIN FACT-FILE

Biotin is a water-soluble B-complex vitamin which is important as a co-enzyme in the production of proteins and fats, and the oxidation of carbohydrates and fatty acids. The bacteria in the intestinal tract produce biotin, and small amounts can be stored in the kidneys, adrenal glands, liver, and brain. Other nutrients which work synergistically with biotin include other B-complex vitamins and vitamin C.

FOOD SOURCE GUIDE

The foods are listed in approximate descending order but nutrient levels, especially of fruit and vegetables, can vary. Where the foods are grown, and the way they are grown, handled, stored and prepared determines their actual nutrient content.

Brewer's yeast and yeast extract
Egg yolk
Oats
Wheat bran and wheatgerm
Fish
Liver and other meat
Wholegrain brown rice
Dairy products
Fresh vegetables
Nuts
Molasses

FACTORS WHICH MAY RAISE REQUIREMENTS

Alcohol
Antibiotics
Large intake of raw egg white*
Oestrogens
Sulphur drugs
Urinary tract anti-infectives

DEFICIENCY SYMPTOMS

Anaemia
Depression
Dermatitis
Increased blood cholesterol levels
Insomnia
Loss of appetite
Muscle aches and pains
Nausea or vomiting
Pallor of the skin
Sore mouth and lips

* Raw egg white contains avidin which is antagonistic to biotin. Avidin is destroyed by heat, so cooked eggs do not have this effect.

OVERDOSE

There is very little available information on this, but taking large quantities of biotin without the other B-complex vitamins can unbalance them and lead to disorders caused by their deficiencies.

ORAL CONTRACEPTIVES AND BIOFLAVONOIDS

It is possible that bioflavonoids are decreased by the use of oral contraceptives, in much the same way as their co-nutrient, vitamin C. Bioflavonoids are important to Pill users as they work with vitamin C in maintaining the health and strength of blood vessels, particularly capilliaries, and some may help prevent blood platelet stickiness. If the diet does not contain foods high in bioflavonoids, or if other factors occur which could decrease them (see: *Factors which may increase requirements* in this section), it may be necessary to supplement up to 100mg, three times a day.

BIOFLAVONOID FACT-FILE

The bioflavonoids are sometimes called flavones, and derive their name from the Latin word *flavus* meaning yellow. They may also be called vitamin P, because of their effect on the permeability of capillaries. Bioflavonoids are a group of water-soluble substances which comprise a number of factors including hesperidin, myrecetin, nobiletin, rutin, tangeritin and quercetin. Vitamin P was first discovered in the white part of citrus fruits, and the flavonoids are responsible for making the yellow and orange colour in citrus fruits. Bioflavonoids and vitamin C work synergistically and are usually found together in foods, and as co-nutrients in vitamin C supplements. Absorption takes place in the intestinal tract. Bioflavonoids are destroyed by boiling and by exposure to air.

FOOD SOURCE GUIDE

The foods are listed in approximate descending order but nutrient levels, especially of fruit and vegetables, can vary. Where the foods are grown, and the way they are grown, handled, stored and prepared determines their actual nutrient content.

Skin and pith of citrus fruit*
Rosehips
Grapes
Apricots
Cherries
Blackcurrants
Plums
Papaya
Green peppers
Blackberries
Tomatoes
Cantaloupe melon
Broccoli
Cabbage
Buckwheat**

FACTORS WHICH MAY RAISE REQUIREMENTS

Aspirin and NSAIs
Diuretics
Exposure to petrol fumes
Oestrogens
Stress

DEFICIENCY SYMPTOMS

Bleeding gums
Easy bleeding or bruising
Small areas of bleeding under the skin

* The entire bioflavonoid complex is found in the whole of the lemon, including the juice.
** The green, immature buckwheat plant contains the highest amount of rutin.

OVERDOSE

No information found.

ORAL CONTRACEPTIVES AND CHOLINE

Oral contraceptives can decrease choline, so if a balanced diet is not eaten or if other factors occur which decrease choline (see: *Factors which may increase requirements* in this section), it may be necessary to supplement up to 250mg a day. As with all B vitamins, choline should be taken as part of the B-complex in order to prevent the symptoms of other B group deficiencies occuring.

CHOLINE FACT-FILE

Choline is a member of the water soluble B-complex vitamins. It is part of a group of fats known as phospholipids which are found in both animal and plant cells and it can be synthesized in the body by the interaction of B_{12} and folic acid with methionine. Choline, combined with fatty acids and phosphoric acid within the liver, forms lecithin. Other nutrients which work synergistically with choline include other B-complex vitamins, especially inositol and B_{12}, vitamin A, linoleic acid, manganese and zinc.

FOOD SOURCE GUIDE

The foods are listed in approximate descending order but nutrient levels, especially of fruit and vegetables, can vary. Where the foods are grown, and the way they are grown, handled, stored and prepared determines their actual nutrient content.

Lecithin
Egg yolk
Beef liver, heart and steak
Wheatgerm
Brewer's yeast
Whole oats
Nuts, beans and peas
Corn or maize

Citrus fruit
Soya flour
Green, leafy, and root vegetables
Bananas

FACTORS WHICH MAY RAISE REQUIREMENTS
Alcohol
Diabetes
Diuretics

DEFICIENCY SYMPTOMS
Fatty deposits in the liver
High blood cholesterol levels
Increased susceptibility to infection
Kidney disorders
Nerve degeneration

OVERDOSE

Large doses of choline over a prolonged period of time can increase B_6 requirements. If you supplement choline on a daily basis, primarily from soya lecithin, it would be wise to include plenty of mineral-rich foods in the diet, especially those high in calcium and magnesium. This is because soya lecithin is high in phosphorus and may upset the body's mineral balance. Taking large quantities of choline without the other B-complex vitamins can unbalance them and lead to disorders caused by their deficiencies.

ORAL CONTRACEPTIVES AND INOSITOL

No information has been found regarding the loss or destruction of inositol by oral contraceptives, but inositol works with choline in the control of blood cholesterol so it is wise to include plenty of inositol in the diet, especially if inositol is decreased by other factors listed in this section.

INOSITOL FACT-FILE

Inositol is a member of the water-soluble B-complex vitamins. It is found in both animal and plant tissues and in cereals. The body's intestinal bacteria are able to produce inositol from glucose. Other nutrients which work synergistically with vitamin A include other B-complex vitamins, especially choline, linoleic acid, manganese and zinc.

FOOD SOURCE GUIDE

The foods are listed in approximate descending order but nutrient levels, especially of fruit and vegetables, can vary. Where the foods are grown, and the way they are grown, handled, stored and prepared determines their actual nutrient content.

Soya lecithin
Beef heart
Liver
Wheatgerm
Whole grains
Nuts
Molasses
Bananas and citrus fruit
Brewer's yeast
Peas and beans
Soya flour
Green, leafy vegetables

FACTORS WHICH MAY RAISE REQUIREMENTS

Alcohol
Diuretics
Lactation
Large consumption of coffee
Pregnancy

DEFICIENCY SYMPTOMS

Fatty accumulations in the liver and other organs, or the vascular system.

OVERDOSE

No information has been found on actual overdose symptoms, however, taking large quantities of inositol without the other B-complex vitamins can unbalance them and lead to disorders caused by their deficiencies.

Note: If you supplement inositol primarily from soya lecithin, on a daily basis, it would be wise to include plenty of mineral-rich foods in the diet, especially those high in calcium and magnesium. This is because soya lecithin is high in phosphorus, and may upset the body's mineral balance.

ORAL CONTRACEPTIVES AND VITAMIN C

Oral contraceptives can deplete vitamin C, possibly by causing the body to break it down more rapidly than is normal. If the diet does not contain plenty of fresh fruit and vegetables or if other factors occur which deplete vitamin C (see: *Factors which may raise requirements* in this section), it may be necessary to supplement up to 200mg of vitamin C with bioflavonoids twice a day. *It is very important not to take more than 400mg of vitamin C daily* as doses higher than this can increase the bioavailability of oestrogen in the body. This has the effect of changing a low-dose Pill to a higher-dose Pill and may lead to an increase in oestrogen-related side-effects, including raised susceptibility to thrombosis. When vitamin C supplementation is withdrawn, it must be done extremely slowly, i.e., gradually reduced over a period of 10 to 14 days. If it is decreased too rapidly, there is the chance of break-through bleeding occuring. This is because the reaction is similar to changing to a lower-dose Pill and it could result in pregnancy.

VITAMIN C FACT-FILE

Vitamin C is also known as ascorbic acid. Calcium ascorbate is a mineral-based supplemental form of vitamin C and ascorbyl palmitate is a fat-soluble supplement. Vitamin C occurs in food and supplements, other than palmitate, as a water-soluble vitamin. It is easily destroyed by heat, light, air and oxidization. It can also be destroyed if vegetables are cooked in iron or copper with baking soda. Very little vitamin C is destroyed when foods are quick-frozen, but it is lost into cooking water. Most animals manufacture their own vitamin C, but humans are not able to do so and must rely on dietary sources. Vitamin C is absorbed from the gastro-intestinal tract into the blood stream and eliminated via the urine and perspiration. It is only stored in the body to a limited extent. Other nutrients which work synergistically with vitamin C include bioflavonoids, vitamin A, calcium and magnesium.

FOOD SOURCE GUIDE

All fruit and vegetables contain some vitamin C, but some of the higher sources are listed below. The foods are listed in approximate descending order but nutrient levels, especially of fruit and vegetables, can vary. Where the foods are grown, and the way they are grown, handled, stored and prepared, determines their actual nutrient content.

Rosehips
Blackcurrants
Fresh or tinned guavas
Papaya
Parsley
Kale
Horseradish
Green peppers
Melons
Brussels sprouts and sprout tops
Lemons
Watercress
Strawberries
Cabbage
Oranges and other citrus fruit
Fresh gooseberries and blackcurrants

FACTORS WHICH MAY RAISE REQUIREMENTS
Alcohol
Antacids

Antibiotics
Anticonvulsants
Antihistamines
Aspirin and other painkillers
Baking soda
Barbiturates
Cortisone
Dental surgery
Diabetes
Exposure to pollution (especially petrol fumes)
High fever
Injury
Menstruation
Oestrogens
Petrol fumes
Smoking
Strenuous physical activity
Stress
Sulphur drugs
Surgery

DEFICIENCY SYMPTOMS

Abnormal bruising or bleeding
Anaemia
Impaired digestion
Increased susceptibility to infection
Irritability
Joint or muscle pains and swelling
Loose teeth
Shortness of breath
Slow wound and fracture healing
Swollen, red or bleeding gums
Weakness

OVERDOSE

Taking more than 400mg of vitamin C daily while using oral contraceptives can increase the risk of side-effects. Doses larger than 400mg should not be taken immediately after discontinuing the Pill, and it is best to let 20 days lapse before increasing the amount being taken. Taking over 750mg of vitamin C a day can lead to side-effects such as a sore tongue, slight burning during urination, nausea, abdominal cramps, loose bowel movements or skin rashes in some people. It can also cause loss of vitamin B_{12}. Because large amounts of vitamin C can precipitate urates, those with gout or kidney stones should discuss its use with a doctor or natural practitioner.

ORAL CONTRACEPTIVES AND VITAMIN E

No information regarding the depletion of vitamin E by oral contraceptives is available, but this nutrient may help in the prevention of blood clots. It may be wise to supplement up to 100iu a day, though doses should not exceed this, as larger amounts can be mildly antagonistic to oestrogen and this may decrease the Pill's effectiveness. (See the important warning under *Overdose* in this section.)

VITAMIN E FACT-FILE

Vitamin E is a fat-soluble vitamin made up of seven compounds called tocopherols, the most active of which is alpha tocopherol. Vitamin E can be listed on supplements as d-alpha which is natural, or dl-alpha which is synthetic. Although vitamin E is fat-soluble, a dry, water-soluble, synthetic form is available as a supplement.

Vitamin E is destroyed by cooking in open pans, and particularly by deep frying. Some may also be lost during commercial deep-freezing. Absorption of vitamin E takes place in the intestines with the help of bile salts and it is found in the liver, fat-storing tissues, muscles such as the heart, and the adrenal, pituitary and sex glands. Excess vitamin E is excreted in the urine. Other nutrients which work synergistically with vitamin E include selenium, vitamins A, B-complex, C and F, manganese, zinc, and sulphur-containing amino acids.

FOOD SOURCE GUIDE

The foods are listed in approximate descending order but nutrient levels
often vary. Where the foods are grown, and the way they are grown,
handled, stored and prepared, determines their actual nutrient content.
Cold-pressed vegetable oils retain more vitamin E than solvent or heat-
processed oils.

Wheatgerm oil
Safflower oil
Soya oil
Other vegetable oils
Wheatgerm
Whole grains
Egg yolk
Sesame seeds, oil and tahini
Sunflower seeds and oil
Avocado
Brown rice
Dark green leafy vegetables
Salmon

FACTORS WHICH MAY RAISE REQUIREMENTS

Diabetes*
High consumption of refined foods
High intake of fats and rancid oils
High intake of polyunsaturated oils
Infections
Lipid-reducing drugs
Liquid paraffin and other laxatives
Malabsorption disorders
Medical treatment with oxygen
Pollutants, including lead

* Insulin-dependent diabetics must consult a doctor before taking vitamin
E, as the insulin dose may need to be adjusted in accordance with the
amount of the vitamin taken.

Pregnancy and lactation
Strenuous activity
Stress

DEFICIENCY SYMPTOMS

Fatigue or decreased energy
Irritability
Leg cramps
Muscle weakness
Possible decrease in fertility

OVERDOSE

Unless under supervision, do not take more than 100iu of vitamin E daily. Large doses may have mild anti-oestrogen activity and could affect the Pill's action. Actual toxicity symptoms are rare at daily doses of up to 600iu but larger doses may cause muscle weakness, fatigue, nausea or diarrhoea.

WARNING

*If you have rheumatic heart disease, mitral valve prolapse or are taking certain heart medicines, vitamin E should **not** be taken in supplement form except under supervision. If you are susceptible to high blood pressure, vitamin E can be taken in supplement form, but **must** be started at a very low dosage and gradually increased. Again, this is best done under supervision. If you are taking digitalis drugs, beta-blockers, or other medicines for the heart, it is important that you consult your doctor before taking vitamin E supplements. Vitamin E should not be taken in doses over 600iu a day without supervision.*

ORAL CONTRACEPTIVES AND COPPER

Oral contraceptives can raise blood copper levels, possibly by increasing its absorption in the intestines and accelerating the liver's production of a copper-binding protein. Elevated levels of copper can result in reduced zinc levels, interference with calcium and vitamin D metabolism, and may also raise the need for vitamin C. Because of this, a balanced diet is vitally important to replace the nutrient losses.

COPPER FACT-FILE

Copper is a trace mineral which is found in all the tissues of the body. A high concentration is found, first, in the liver and, secondly, in the brain. It is also found in the muscles, bones, heart and glands. Copper is absorbed in the stomach and upper intestine. It is excreted by the liver via the bile and the faeces and a small amount is also lost in the urine.

SOME SIGNIFICANT COPPER SOURCES

These are some of the higher copper sources, listed in approximate descending order.

Oysters
Whelks
Crab
Shrimp
Liver
Brewer's yeast
Olives
Lentils
Nuts
Cod
Poultry
Breads and grains
Tea
Cocoa and chocolate
Curry powder
Meat
Peanuts

OTHER SOURCES

Copper can be ingested from copper water pipes, pesticides, fungicides and copper cooking utensils.

FACTORS WHICH MAY DECREASE COPPER

Excessive phytic acid intake
Malabsorption disorders
Prolonged diarrhoea
Some medical treatments, such as dialysis

OVERDOSE

Copper toxicity symptoms include abdominal pain, nausea, vomiting, diarrhoea, mental disorders and anaemia. It is extremely rare that this occurs, but raised blood-copper levels may be found where the following occur:

Abnormal copper metabolism
Epilepsy
Some heart disorders
High blood cholesterol
Hyperactivity in children
Oral contraceptive use
Rheumatoid arthritis
Some types of schizophrenia
Zinc deficiency states

ORAL CONTRACEPTIVES AND MANGANESE

Oral contraceptives can indirectly decrease manganese because they increase copper levels which, in abnormal amounts, can decrease manganese. If a balanced diet is not eaten, and if other factors occur which decrease manganese (see: *Factors which may raise requirements* in this section), it may be necessary to supplement by up to 9mg daily.

MANGANESE FACT-FILE

Manganese is an essential trace mineral required by the brain and nervous system. It is absorbed slowly from the small intestine and a high concentration is stored in the bones, kidneys, liver, pancreas and heart. Manganese is excreted via the bile, faeces, urine and perspiration. Other nutrients which work synergistically with manganese include vitamins B_1 and E, calcium and phosphorus.

FOOD SOURCE GUIDE

The foods are listed in approximate descending order but nutrient levels, especially of fruit and vegetables, can vary. Where the foods are grown, and the way they are grown, handled, stored and prepared, determines their actual nutrient content.

Oats and other whole grains
Wheatgerm
Avocados
Chestnuts
Nuts
Peas
Sesame, pumpkin and sunflower seeds
Olives
Pineapple
Bananas
Blackberries
Watercress
Dulse seaweed
Beetroot
Offal
Green leafy vegetables
Cloves
Ginger
Brewer's yeast
Molasses

Note: Ordinary tea contains a high amount of manganese but this is offset by its high tannin content which prevents manganese absorption.

FACTORS WHICH MAY RAISE REQUIREMENTS

High intake of processed foods
High tannin intake
Large intake of calcium and phosphorus
Low intake of fresh fruit and vegetables

DEFICIENCY SYMPTOMS

Blood-sugar disorders
Convulsions
Ear disorders
Failure of muscle co-ordination

OVERDOSE

Toxicity from dietary intake is rare. The symptoms of poisoning, usually from industrial sources, include weakness, apathy, muscular and movement disorders, loss of appetite, headaches, lung disorders, nerve degeneration similar to Parkinson's disease, tremors and schizophrenic behaviour.

ORAL CONTRACEPTIVES AND ZINC

Zinc levels may be depleted by oral contraceptives so if a balanced diet is not eaten or if other factors occur which deplete zinc (see: *Factors which may raise requirements* in this section), it may be necessary to supplement the diet by up to 30mg of zinc daily. Decreased zinc levels may increase the risk of cardiovascular disease.

ZINC FACT-FILE

Zinc is a water-soluble trace element. The body only contains about half a teaspoon of zinc. It is essential to many of the body's functions and is found in almost all tissues, especially the thyroid gland, pancreas, reproductive organs (especially the prostate gland in men), liver, kidney, bones and muscles. It is absorbed in the upper part of the small intestine and excreted in the faeces, urine, sweat and semen. Because zinc is water soluble it may be lost into cooking water.

FOOD SOURCE GUIDE

The foods are listed in approximate descending order but nutrient levels, especially of fruit and vegetables, can vary. Where the foods are grown, and the way they are grown, handled, stored and prepared, determines their actual nutrient content.

Liver
Brewer's yeast
Seafood
Herring
Pumpkin seeds
Wheatgerm
Meat
Eggs and dairy products
Whole grains
Rye bread
Poultry
Nuts
Peas
Other vegetables

FACTORS WHICH MAY RAISE REQUIREMENTS

Breast-feeding
Corticosteroids, long-term or high-dose
Diabetes
Diet high in refined or processed foods
Digitalis drugs
Excessive intake of calcium, copper and iron
Excessive perspiring
Exposure to lead and other pollutants
High alcohol intake
High carbohydrate, low protein intake

High phytic acid intake
Liver and kidney disease
Malabsorption disorders
Oestrogens
Penicillamine chelating agents
Pregnancy
Stress
Thiazide diuretics

Note: If you are vegetarian or vegan, your diet may be high in phytic acid which can decrease your body's absorption of zinc. Fermented foods such as miso contain the enzyme phytase which can offset phytic acid's effects. Sourdough or breads which have risen with yeast do not contain phytic acid, so the zinc in the grains is available to the body.

DEFICIENCY SYMPTOMS

Allergies
Apathy
Bleeding gums
Disorders of the reproductive system
Hair loss or brittle hair
Increased susceptibility to infections
Loss of sense of taste and smell
Post-natal depression
Skin lesions
Slow wound, ulcer or burn healing
Suppressed appetite
White spots on the nails

OVERDOSE

Excess zinc is excreted in the urine. However, no more than 30mg of supplementary zinc should be taken a day, unless it has been recommended by a doctor or practitioner. A high intake of zinc may interfere with copper metabolism and increase the need for foods rich in vitamin A. Although low zinc levels may increase the risk of cardiovascular disease, excessively high doses have been shown to increase cholesterol levels in the body. Researchers have found the amount of zinc which produced this effect was approximately 100mg or more daily, taken for an extended period of time.

Chapter 7

FEELING GOOD
THE NUTRITION EQUATION
PART TWO

A good diet is very important when using oral contraceptives because of its effect on the body's nutritional status. It is well known that the Pill can raise the requirements for vitamin B_6 and zinc, but many other nutrients are affected. It has been shown that a consistently poor diet which is low in nutrients, can result in lowered health, especially in conjunction with Pill use.

Since a good diet is the basis of good health, it is necessary to consider its importance seriously when using the Pill. The information in this chapter can be used to plan daily diets, choose more healthy and nutritious foods, and decrease foods and drinks which may increase nutrient loss or contribute to side-effects such as cardiovascular disorders or weight gain. Decreasing the consumption of some foods while choosing to eat more of others can help to protect your present and future health.

PLANNING THE DIET

A little planning can go a long way towards achieving a varied and balanced diet. Cutting down on meat and dairy products can theoretically leave more room in the budget for a greater variety of vegetables and fruit. Many stores now sell organically grown or exotic produce and there are more additive-free, low-salt, low-sugar and low-fat foods to choose from. If you eat meat or eggs, it can be worthwhile to buy free-range eggs and meat from naturally reared animals — if your budget allows it. Firstly, this helps to support more humane treatment of livestock. Secondly, until the use of hormones in the breeding of farm animals is controlled, an unknown amount of steroids are finding their way into meat. Oral contraceptives contain steroid hormones and, although there is almost no evidence available as to the safety or danger of these residues in meat, it does seem wise to try to avoid all extra sources.

While taking oral contraceptives there are some foods which are best reduced or left out of the diet completely. Oestrogens in the combined Pill may cause some people to retain water so a diet high in salt may contribute to symptoms such as swollen ankles, legs or fingers. It is also wise to limit consumption of refined sugar and carbohydrates because they can contribute to the blood-sugar disorders which some women experience when taking the Pill. Refined sugar, alcohol and other 'empty' carbohydrates may also contribute indirectly to raised blood cholesterol because excessive consumption can increase the levels of triglycerides or blood fats in the body. Lowering fat intake can decrease the total calories consumed. Eating more alkaline foods such as fresh vegetables and fruit, and less acid foods, as well as fewer calories, offers health benefits including possible protection against breast disease, and increased immune response.

SATURATED FATS, CHOLESTEROL, AND THE CARDIOVASCULAR CONNECTION

Cholesterol is an important fat-like substance which is manufactured in the liver and found throughout the body. It performs many vital functions, including acting as a precursor in the manufacture of various sex hormones. When the liver produces too much cholesterol or the diet consistently contains high amounts of saturated fats, cholesterol can begin to build up on the inside of arteries and may eventually lead to cardiovascular disorders.

Saturated fats are fat molecules filled with hydrogen. When these are eaten in large quantities, they can raise the level of cholesterol in the blood stream. Some of the highest amounts are found in foods such as fats which are solid at room temperature — full-fat milk products, fatty meats and hydrogenated oils. Eggs are often eliminated from cholesterol-reduced diets because the yolk contains a relatively high percentage of this fat. However, egg yolk is balanced with lecithin which is nature's fat emulsifier and when eggs are lightly poached or soft boiled, the benefits of heat-sensitive lecithin remain. It is only by hard-boiling, overcooking or using eggs in baking that their cholesterol content can become a problem. An American poultry firm has found that, by feeding their hens a better diet and improving their housing, the hens laid eggs with a lower cholesterol content. This could be another good reason for choosing free-range eggs laid by hens with a more natural diet.

Oral contraceptives can lead to an increased level of the blood fats, cholesterol and triglycerides, which have been linked with cardiovascular disease. By reducing the amount of saturated fats, alcohol, refined sugar, and carbohydrates in the diet, levels of dietary cholesterol and triglycerides may be kept under control. For more details see the chapter on natural remedies.

PRESERVING THE NUTRIENTS IN FOOD

Even the best-planned diets are prey to deficiencies, especially since the way foods are grown, stored, transported, displayed or processed can leave them with far fewer nutrients than nature intended. Lifestyle affects the way foods are digested, absorbed and used. Rushing around and eating on the run or in an environment filled with noise and stress takes its toll. Factors such as smoking, alcohol, and certain medicines also contribute to nutrient loss.

In order to preserve the vitamin and mineral content of vegetables, they should be lightly pressure cooked or steamed, rather than boiled. The water should be saved to make soups, broths or savoury drinks. Many people add baking soda to cooking water to make vegetables appear more attractive and, although appearance is an important aspect of food preparation, baking soda can cause nutrient loss and should be avoided. Eating certain foods whole or raw cuts down losses from peeling and cooking. It is always best to buy really fresh-looking fruit and vegetables as, the more wilted they appear, the greater the nutrient depletion. Wash vegetables quickly and try to avoid soaking them but, if you have to prepare them ahead of time, it helps to decrease vitamin loss if they are covered and chilled. Peel vegetables very thinly and cut them as close as possible to the time that they will be cooked.

Try taking time for eating, play some quiet, restful music, relax and chew the food well — as an added bonus you may be surprised that you feel like eating a little less food and feel more satisfied afterwards. Presentation of the meal is also important, so choose different coloured foods, and 'design' them on your plate. Try to avoid meals spiced with arguments, tension or noise.

ALUMINIUM SAUCEPANS

We all need a minute amount of aluminium in our bodies, but because we ingest so much it can be a threat to health. Aluminium cookware is a source of this metal as it can leach into the food which is cooked in it. Anyone using aluminium saucepans is probably aware that acid foods such as tomatoes turn the pan black when they are cooked in it. This reaction is indicative of aluminium being leached from the pan into the food. Acid foods are the worst offenders.

Stainless steel seems to be the safest cookware, but if this is too expensive, glassware may be a safer alternative to aluminium. Iron skillets or frying pans are considered to be safe.

SAFE STORAGE

Plasticizers may leach from plastic containers into foods and this can be harmful to health, so it is always best to avoid storing food in plastic tubs or dishes. If this is difficult, ensure that food has completely cooled down before putting it into the container. Some brands of cling film still contain plasticizers which migrate into food, so it is best to avoid using cling film in the microwave, or with fatty or hot foods.

FOOD FRAMEWORK

The foods listed here have been classified by taking into account their nutrient, salt, cholesterol, refined sugar and caffeine content.

RECOMMENDED FOOD AND BEVERAGES

Planning the diet using mainly fresh, whole and unprocessed foods can help to ensure that your body is provided with a good supply of the nutrients and fibre it needs. The list which follows has been compiled to give you an idea of the variety of foods to choose from.

Food
Variety of whole grains
Variety of fresh vegetables
Variety of fresh fruit
Wholemeal bread such as pumpernickle, corn or wheat
Organic rice cakes
'Live' yoghurt
Variety of fresh fish
Wholegrain buckwheat or wheat pasta
Legumes or beans
Sesame tahini and other seed or nut butters
Fresh seasoning herbs
Virgin, cold-pressed olive oil
Other cold-pressed oils
Tofu
Lean meats
Low-fat cheeses
Sugar-free jams
Free-range eggs
Sunflower, pumpkin and sesame seeds
Chestnuts
Sea vegetables
Un-sorbated, un-sulphured dried fruit
Avocados
Small amount of fresh nuts

Beverages
Spring water with a squeeze of lemon
Mineral water
Coffee substitutes
Low-fat milk
Soya milk
Herbal teas such as lemongrass, peppermint, rosehip, fennel, chamomile

Spreads

These can include sesame tahini, almond, hazelnut or sunflower butter, vegetable paste spreads, vegetarian spreads (without hydrogenated oils), tofu spreads, Vitazell or Vitaseig (unhydrogenated margarines available from health food shops) or a little slightly salted butter.

Desserts or snacks

   Fresh fruit
   Yoghurt
   Baked or stewed fruit
   Pumpkin or sunflower seeds
   Wholegrain biscuits sweetened only with fruit juice

Seasonings, condiments and stocks

Include fresh or dried herbs such as basil, coriander, oregano, chives, rosemary, thyme, garlic and ginger. Season grains, stews, bakes, etc. with Vecon, soya sauce, miso, or vegetable stock cubes. For extra zest, try a little organic horseradish sauce or Worcestershire sauce (Ask at your health food shop for one that doesn't contain sugar, salt and malt vinegar.) Sugar-free chutneys and cranberry sauce are available at a growing number of stores, and it is possible to find wholegrain mustard made with cider vinegar and honey.

POOR FOODS

It is not recommended to include a high percentage of the following foods in the diet, especially when using oral contraceptives.

   Refined sugar and foods containing it
   Fried foods, including snack foods
   Table salt and highly salted foods
   Bleached white flour
   White bread, cakes, biscuits, etc.
   Processed foods
   Canned vegetables
   Highly boiled vegetables
   Vegetables cooked with bicarbonate of soda

Overcooked or burned foods
Caffeine
Foods high in saturated fats such as cream or gold top and full
fat milk, hydrogenated oils, high fat cheeses, butter, margarine,
suet, lard and dripping, fatty meats, meat skin and meat
products, biscuits, cakes, pastries, chocolate.

DAILY FOOD PLANS

The main points taken into account in the food plans are:

● The importance of a variety of whole, fresh foods to supply important
enzymes and nutrients.

● Keeping salt, sugar, preservatives, artificial colouring, and cholesterol
to a minimum.

● The minimum of repetition, especially of food such as wheat, milk
and eggs with a high potential for causing an allergic reaction. This
is because food allergies can sometimes develop during the use of
oral contraceptives.

● The inclusion of foods high in fibre.

● The use of less meat without decreasing protein intake.

● That the lunches and dinners are interchangeable; because, although
it can be healthier to eat your heaviest meal at lunchtime rather than
in the evening, work or lifestyle often make this difficult.

● The inclusion of sources of B_{12}, both vegetarian and non-vegetarian.
However, vegans and vegetarians who avoid eggs and dairy products
should check with the section on B_{12} in chapter six, to ensure that
enough foods containing B_{12} are eaten daily.

● Bread is used as a blanket term for loaves made from corn, rye, and
rice, as well as wheat.

If certain food combinations upset your digestive system and well-being,
avoid eating protein and carbohydrates together and increase the amount

of leafy vegetables eaten with protein foods.

Some recipes are included at the end of the chapter, but you should refer to a good wholefood or vegetarian cookery book for more recipes and ideas. Suggestions for snacks and desserts can be found in the first part of this chapter.

Nutritional supplements are optional — guidelines on what to take and when to take it are given at the end of this chapter.

DAY ONE

Breakfast
Low sugar, low sodium wholegrain cereal with nuts or seeds, fresh fruit, and vegetarian or skimmed milk. Wholegrain toast. Choose a beverage from the list which appears in part one of this chapter.

Lunch or dinner
Grilled or poached fish, or vegetarian burgers. Serve with runner or broad beans and spring greens, baked or new potatoes. Choose a beverage from the list which appears in the first part of this chapter.

Dinner or lunch
Home-made soup with oatcakes and a large mixed salad with sliced avocado or sardines or pilchards. Choose a beverage from the list which appears in part one of this chapter.

DAY TWO

Breakfast
Baked beans with no added sugar on whole grain toast such as rye pumpernickel, or omelette with cottage cheese, red or green peppers and toast. Serve with bean sprouts or alfalfa sprouts. Choose a beverage from the list which appears in the first part of this chapter.

Lunch or dinner
Baked chicken or tofu bake with broccoli and carrots and/or baked pumpkin or squash. Serve with cooked buckwheat. Choose a beverage

from the list which appears in part one of this chapter.

Dinner or lunch
Rice cake pizza served with a mixed vegetable salad and natural dressing.
Choose a beverage from the list which appears in part one of this chapter.

DAY THREE

Breakfast
Hot porridge oats or oatbran cereal made with soya or skimmed cow's
milk. Sprinkle with ground sunflower and pumpkin seeds, and chopped
banana. A little sugar-free jam can be mixed in to give a sweet flavour,
or carob powder or sugar-free carob drops can add a flavour which is
similar to chocolate. Choose a beverage from the list which appears in
part one of this chapter.

Lunch or dinner
Bean or lean meat casserole with french beans, cauliflower and new
potatoes or grilled potato slices, or savoy cabbage, baked parsnips, carrots
and sweet potato. Choose a beverage from the list which appears in the
first part of this chapter.

Dinner or lunch
Soup and rice cakes followed by a large mixed salad with dressing, and
grilled vegetarian sausages, vegetarian tofu burgers, or pilchards or
sardines. Choose a beverage from the list which appears in part one of
this chapter.

DAY FOUR

Breakfast
Millet cooked in water and apple juice, served with stewed fruit and
natural yoghurt, or grapefruit followed by rye or rice cereal with yoghurt
or fruit juice, sprinkled with fresh or dried fruit, sunflower and pumpkin
seeds, or nuts. Choose a beverage from the list which appears in part
one of this chapter.

Lunch or dinner
Buckwheat spaghetti or wholewheat pasta with tahini and soya sauce
or no-sugar, low-salt tomato sauce. Serve with courgettes, kale or sprout
tops, and sweetcorn. Choose a beverage from the list which appears in
the first part of this chapter.

Dinner or lunch
Vegetarian marinated tofu kebabs or lean-meat kebabs on a bed of brown
rice seasoned with saffron or vegetable stock, or rolled into sheets of
nori seaweed. Include a watercress and mushroom salad with dressing.
Choose a beverage from the list which appears in the first part of this
chapter.

DAY FIVE

Breakfast
Fruit and nut muffins with yoghurt drink. Choose a beverage from the
list which appears in part one of this chapter.

Lunch or dinner
Buckwheat pancakes filled with beans, leeks, mushrooms and sauce or
chicken in savoury sauce. Serve with artichoke and carrots or brussels
sprouts and carrots, and new or baked potatoes. Choose a beverage from
the list which appears in part one of this chapter.

Dinner or lunch
Soup and cornbread. Quiche with mixed vegetable salad. Choose a
beverage from the list which appears in the first part of this chapter.

DAY SIX

Breakfast
Lightly poached or soft boiled eggs with rye pumpernickel bread or toast
served with watercress. Choose a beverage from the list which appears
in part one of this chapter.

Lunch or dinner
Baked or grilled fish with fresh lemon juice, or vegetarian curry. Serve with broccoli, peas and small, whole boiled onions, and kasha. Choose a beverage from the list which appears in part one of this chapter.

Dinner or lunch
Wholewheat pitta bread spread with sesame tahini and stuffed with a variety of fresh salad vegetables and grated low-fat cow's milk or vegetarian cheese or cottage cheese. Season with fresh chopped herbs such as coriander, basil or oregano, and use a spread of your choice. Choose a beverage from the list which appears in part one of this chapter.

DAY SEVEN

Breakfast
Yoghurt topped with stewed fruit, granola and chopped nuts or seeds. Choose a beverage from the list which appears in part one of this chapter.

Lunch or dinner
Vegetarian lasagne, or grilled steak, tomatoes and mushrooms. Serve with runner or green beans, sweetcorn or asparagus. Choose a beverage from the list which appears in part one of this chapter.

Dinner or lunch
Salmon or tuna salad, or baked lentil loaf. Serve with boiled new potatoes or grilled potato slices. Choose a beverage from the list which appears in part one of this chapter.

SIMPLE RECIPES

All of these recipes can be made in larger quantities and frozen to be eaten later.

BROWN RICE

Brown rice comes in short, medium or long-grain varieties. Short-grain is stickier so it tends to be a little thicker when cooked. Sweet rice is the most starchy and is often used for desserts. Try to buy organically grown rice as it tends to be quite a heavily chemical treated grain. Brown, unpolished rice is an excellent source of B-complex vitamins and vitamin B_1 was first isolated from rice polishings in 1926.

See Thorsons' range of cookery books for brown rice recipes, or try the following suggestions:

To cook brown rice, use a heavy bottomed, non-aluminium, saucepan. For both long-grain and short-grain rice use three parts water to one part rice. Medium-grain rice needs two parts water to one part rice. If you use a pressure cooker you will need slightly less water. Bring the water to the boil and add the rice, bring back to the boil, stir and allow to simmer slowly with the lid on the pan, avoiding stirring. When the rice has absorbed all the water it is ready — this may take 20-25 minutes. Rice can be mixed with other grains and vegetables and used as a savoury dish, or for breakfasts and desserts.

BUCKWHEAT OR KASHA

Despite the name, buckwheat is not a member of the wheat family. It is gluten-free grain which contains very little sodium. It is available whole, toasted or un-toasted, and is high in potassium, phosphorus, calcium and contains B-complex vitamins. It is a good source of protein, which is closer to animal protein than any other plant. Rutin is found in the green, immature buckwheat plant. To make buckwheat into a savoury dish, use a thick bottomed non-aluminium pan and use one part grain to two parts water. Add vegetable stock and simmer for about 15 minutes, until tender. Buckwheat combined with millet makes a good stuffing for peppers or cabbage leaves. It can also be mixed with vegetables and makes very good curry. Buckwheat is a vegetarian staple and many more recipes can be found in any good vegetarian or wholefood cookery book.

GRILLED OR BAKED POTATO SLICES

Cut almost-cooked boiled potatoes into thin slices, then bake or grill until lightly browned. Serve topped with chopped chives.

MILLET

Millet is a low-gluten grain which is very easily digested. It is a good source of protein and contains a number of B-complex vitamins and minerals, especially potassium. Try the following suggestions. To make millet, use a thick bottomed non-aluminium pan. For breakfast cereal, use one part grain to two parts water, fruit juice or milk and add cinnamon and maple syrup or honey to taste. As a savoury dish, simmer one part millet to two parts water and a little vegetable stock. Mix with dill and vegetables. Millet can be ground into flour and used in similar ways to corn or maize flour.

RICE-CAKE PIZZAS

Spread rice cakes with a little sugar-free, low-salt tomato sauce or purée, then cover with chopped vegetables such as mushrooms, peppers and olives and cover with grated mozzarella or cheddar cheese and chopped basil and oregano. Grill until lightly browned.

STEWED OR RECONSTITUTED FRUIT

Gently simmer pears or apples with cloves and cinnamon in fruit juice, until tender. To make reconstituted dried fruit, place dried fruit in a glass basin, pour boiling water over it and add cloves or cinnamon. If it requires sweetening, add a little concentrated fruit juice or a little honey. Cover and leave overnight in a refrigerator or cool place. Serve cold, or warm before eating.

YOGHURT DRINK

Blend natural yoghurt with a little honey and fruit, or no-sugar-added jam to taste. Refrigerate for about ten minutes before serving.

GENERAL SUPPLEMENT PROGRAMME

Supplement	With or after b'fast	With or after lunch	With or after dinner	Before bed	Notes
Vitamin B-complex (25mg)	1	1			
Vitamin B$_6$ (25mg)		1			
Vitamin C with bioflavonoids (200mg)	1	1			
Vitamin E 100iu	1				
Multiple mineral containing up to 30mg of zinc				1	Avoid mineral supplements containing copper
Lecithin granules	3 tsps				
Acidophilus powder	1 tsps				

Please note that supplements should only be taken after discussion with your doctor.

Chapter 8

DISCONTINUING THE PILL

It is generally recommended that combined oral contraceptives should be discontinued when a woman reaches 35 (if she is a smoker) or 45 (if she is a non-smoker) because the risk of stroke increases with age. The progestogen-only, or mini-Pill, is often suggested as an alternative.

When deciding to stop the Pill all you have to do is discontinue your daily Pill taking routine — preferably at the end of a pack, although you can stop at any point. However, stopping closer to the middle of a packet may bring on your period early and this can increase the chance of pregnancy if you have had sexual intercourse within a few days. Doctors and clinics recommend that three months should elapse after using oral contraceptives before trying to become pregnant. This allows time for the body's hormonal and nutritional status to return to normal. (For more information see: *Pregnancy after the pill*, at the end of this chapter.) During this time, barrier methods of contraception are recommended over the temperature and cervical mucus methods, as these rely on monitoring the body's menstrual cycle, which may not be reliable for up to three months after stopping the Pill.

If you have any doubt about discontinuing oral contraceptives contact your local family planning clinic or your GP for more help and advice. (Remember, you can contact another GP for family planning advice if you don't wish to talk to your usual doctor.)

RETURN OF OVULATION AND MENSTRUATION

Most women experience the return of menstruation within three months of stopping the Pill although the time lapse for conception is generally a little longer after discontinuing the Pill than after non-hormonal methods of contraception. Other possible reasons for delay are a pre-Pill history of irregular menstruation, and there is also evidence that women who are underweight may have a longer delay in the return of their periods after the Pill has been stopped. The hormones in oral contraceptives suppress the activity of the hypothalamus and in around 2 per cent of women this may account for a prolonged absence of ovulation and menstruation after using the Pill.

Only a very small percentage of women fail to start their period within six months of stopping the Pill and, although this should not be cause for undue alarm, the absence of menstruation may be due to disorders which require medical attention. Common reasons include disorders of the ovaries or pituitary gland, or failure of ovulation to be triggered — a problem which tends to be more widespread among Pill users than non-users. Because six months absence of menstruation may indicate a disorder which requires medical attention, it is very important to contact your doctor if menstruation has not occurred within this time. Progestogens in the Pill can actually reduce the chance of suffering from pelvic inflammatory disease, better known as PID, some cases of which may increase the risk of infertility. For the latest information and research on the Pill it is best to contact your local family planning clinic, the Family Planning Information Service, or talk to your doctor.

Up to 40 per cent of women who fail to ovulate or menstruate post-Pill also notice a clear or milky discharge from the nipple(s). Doctors call this galactorrhoea, or inappropriate lactation. Galactorrhoea can result from the Pill's suppression of a hormone which prevents lactation and it usually subsides when ovulation returns to normal.

If you have any worries at all after stopping the Pill, or if you think you may have become pregnant it is best to check with your local family planning clinic or talk to your doctor.

POST-PILL PMS

If you suffered from PMS before taking the Pill it is likely that you may experience it again when the Pill is discontinued. For some women, the

Pill's hormonal content can actually help this condition while it is being used, but others experience PMS before every withdrawal bleed. For natural help see chapter 5.

SELF-HELP

If your doctor has found no serious medical reason for failure of the menstrual cycle or fertility to return then it may help to begin looking at lifestyle and diet for clues to the problem. You can use the following information to evaluate personal lifestyle and dietary habits which may be contributing to prolonged absence of ovulation and menstruation.

Stress   Stress can be a significant factor in delayed menstruation and even in some fertility problems. Stress and tension are thought to inhibit menstruation by hindering the release of important hormones. They may also interfere with ovulation. Although it is often difficult to avoid stressful situations, it is possible to help your body cope with stress. Stress can increase your body's need for optimum nutrition — especially affected are B-complex vitamins, vitamins C, E and A, minerals such as zinc, calcium, magnesium and potassium. (For more information on food and supplements see chapters 6 and 7). Using relaxation techniques is a way of learning how to deal with stress.

For information about relaxation contact:

Relaxation for Living,
29 Burwood Park Road,
Walton-On-Thames,
Surrey,
KT12 5LH.

They are a registered charity and organize small group relaxation classes throughout the country, or correspondence courses for those out of reach of a teacher. They also publish and distribute self-help leaflets and cassettes. Please send a large stamped, self-addressed envelope for more information.

Smoking

Studies have shown that smoking affects the menstrual cycle and fertility. The negative effect appears to increase with the number of cigarettes smoked daily — the higher the number smoked, the longer it may take to conceive. Smoking is thought to affect the reproductive system through hormonal changes and it is known to increase the need for vitamins E, A and C and the mineral zinc. It may help to try to reduce or stop smoking. If you would like help, you can contact Action on Smoking and Health, a charitable organization which offers help on how to stop smoking. Please send a stamped, addressed envelope with all enquiries to:

Action on Smoking and Health,
5-11 Mortimer Street,
London W1N 7RH.

Acupuncture is often used to help stop smoking, and other natural practitioners may also be able to offer some help.

Alcohol

A high intake of alcohol can increase the body's need for a number of nutrients, especially vitamins such as B-complex, C and a number of minerals, among which is zinc. Alcohol consumed frequently may be enough to tip the nutritional scales too much in the wrong direction for some people. If you are unable to reduce or stop drinking alcohol it can be beneficial to your general health. If you would like some extra help then an alternative/complementary practitioner may be able to assist you.

Exercise

Walking, swimming, cycling and other forms of exercise, preferably in the fresh air, are important for building a strong body and immune system. Moderate exercise is vital for stimulating the digestive system, the glands and circulation, and its importance is often forgotten in connection with the reproductive system. If you find it difficult to exercise in the winter, a rebounder, which is a type of small trampoline, can be used for jogging and other gentle exercises. Bear in mind that excessive exercise (running more than 40 miles a week) can cause ovulation to stop (amenorrhoea).

Nutrition

Eating a diet which consists of a large percentage of refined foods and a low proportion of fresh, wholefoods can sometimes contribute to menstrual and fertility disorders, because of the decreased availability of certain nutrients and enzymes. Taking the Pill can increase the dietary requirements for a number of vitamins and minerals, most notably folic acid, vitamin B_6 and the mineral zinc. These are vital for the health of the reproductive system. Zinc is especially difficult to obtain in adequate amounts from the diet, mainly because of low zinc levels in the soil, and food refining processes which decrease levels even further. Other important nutrients include vitamin A, which is required by the glands and for the production of sex hormones; the B-complex vitamins, which play an important role in the body's hormonal balance; vitamin E, which is important for the production and protection of sex hormones; and vitamin C which is involved in glandular health.

A teaspoonful of virgin, cold-pressed olive oil in the diet every day supplies vitamin F — fatty acids, which have been found essential for reproductive system health. These can apply whether you are taking the Pill, or want to help restore normal reproductive function after discontinuing oral contraception. (For general diet and supplement suggestions see chapters 6 and 7.)

NATURAL PRACTITIONERS

For individual dietary advice or for help with menstrual or fertility disorders, a natural practitioner can be consulted. The following list gives brief descriptions of the treatment some practitioners may offer and can be used as a guide when selecting alternative or complementary help.

Acupuncture   Acupuncture can be used to help balance the whole body including the hormones and glands. It can also be used to help stop smoking and drinking alcohol.

Chiropractic   A chiropractor can adjust your body to help relieve stress, tension and bad posture which may be contributing to your disorder. Chiropractic can also help to free nerve and energy pathways and often a simple adjustment can bring on a late period.

Herbalism   The individual use of specific herbs is often very helpful for disorders of the reproductive system. Certain herbs can influence hormonal levels in the body.

Homoeopathy   Homoeopaths select specific remedies for each individual by considering the whole person, including the personality as well as symptoms, habits, etc. Homoeopathic remedies help the body to initiate the process of healing.

Naturopathy   Naturopathy is a holistic approach to healing which uses a number of methods including water therapy, diet, fresh air, massage, exercise and relaxation to bring about balance and healing.

Osteopathy   Osteopaths seek to restore the correct balance of nerve and energy flow and circulation in the body. Often a simple spinal adjustment can bring on a late menstrual period.

PREGNANCY AFTER THE PILL

It is generally recommended to try to avoid becoming pregnant for three months after discontinuing the Pill. This will allow time for your periods to become normal and for your body to adjust to hormonal and nutritional changes. Most doctors and clinics make this recommendation because the very minimal risk of abnormalities in the child may be increased if conception takes place immediately after stopping the Pill. However, women who do become pregnant while taking, or just after stopping the Pill may be reassured by an estimate made by the Population Council. Their research suggests that only seven out of every 10,000 pregnancies which occured during Pill use may possibly have an abnormality attributable to the Pill.

Approximately 90 per cent of women who have had children, and about 80 per cent of women who have not had children are able to conceive within one year of stopping the Pill and there is very little evidence and, to date, none conclusive, that the Pill can cause irreversible sterility. Research has shown that the only risks to the foetus attributable to former Pill use are nutritional. Folic acid and zinc are both decreased by Pill use and are crucial to normal foetal development so the importance of optimum nutrition, before, during and after pregnancy is vital. If the nutritional guidelines found in chapters 6 and 7 are followed, the risks of nutritional deficiencies may be reduced. Smoking and alcohol both increase requirements for a number of important vitamins and minerals including A, C, and E and zinc, selenium and potassium so it is very important to ensure that your diet contains plenty of foods rich in these nutrients. (For more information see chapters 6 and 7 and *The Medicine Chest* published by Thorsons, 1988.) If supplements are necessary, they should be free from artificial colourings, flavourings, sugar and salt and preferably be derived from natural sources.

Always check with your doctor or Family Planning Association for individual dietary advice, and avoid taking any supplemental vitamins and minerals while you are pregnant, unless advised to do so by a doctor.

FOR MORE HELP

If you would like more information on fertility, contact Foresight, an association which can help couples work out nutritional and environmental problems which may be contributing to infertility or preventing conception. They can also supply the name of a doctor in your area who you can consult. Please send a stamped, self-addressed envelope with all correspondence. Their address is:

Foresight
Association for Preconceptual Care
The Old Vicarage
Church Lane
Witley
Godalming
Surrey, GU8 5PN

For more addresses see the section on family planning and fertility in chapter 9. Your GP can also advise on good pre-conceptual care.

FUTURE HEALTH

Having taken the Pill at some point in life does not seem to affect the menopause. If you have questions about this it is best to contact your local family planning clinic or to speak to your doctor. With the older, higher-dose Pills, the very slight risk of cardiovascular disease or stroke seems to carry over for about six years after discontinuing the Pill. However, it is a lower-risk ratio than for women actually taking the Pill and seems to apply mainly to smokers over 35 who continue to smoke after stopping the Pill. The low-dose Pills which are used now are thought to be even less likely to carry this risk.

By following the dietary suggestions outlined in chapter 7, before, during and after Pill use, it may be possible to improve the chances of better future health.

Chapter 9

SELF-HELP GROUPS

During Pill use there may be questions or problems which arise. This chapter provides details about organizations and associations which may be able to assist you. The associations are listed under explanatory headings to enable you to find the groups which can best deal with your problem.

Family planning clinics are located all over the country in nearly every town and to find your local clinic check in the telephone directory or the Yellow Pages under *Family planning*. Alternatively you can find out the times and addresses of your nearest clinic from the Town Hall, Post Office or your health visitor or contact the Family Planning Information Service. Family planning clinics are run by the NHS and come under the District Health Authorities.

BRITAIN

ALTERNATIVE AND COMPLEMENTARY MEDICAL ASSOCIATIONS

Council for Acupuncture
Suite 1
19a Cavendish Square
London W1M 9AD
Tel 01 409 1440

The Council for Acupuncture is part of the Council for Complementary Medicine and it works towards protecting the public with regard to hygiene and needle sterilization. For copies of the *Code of Practice and Ethics of Acupuncture* and for a register of British acupuncturists, please send £1.50.

Council for Complementary and Alternative Medicine
Suite 1
19a Cavendish Square
London W1M 9AD
Tel 01 409 1440

The Council provides a forum for communication and co-operation between professional bodies representing acupuncture, chiropractic, homoeopathy, medical herbalism, naturopathy, and osteopathy. They will provide the name and address of a practitioner registered with the Council. Please send a stamped, self-addressed envelope with your enquiry.

Institute for Complementary Medicine
21 Portland Place
London W1N 3AF

This is a registered charity which can give information on practitioners and complementary medicine, either on a national or local level. They can also provide details of special courses for medical students, nurses, and other groups. There is a clinic which has a team of highly trained complementary practitioners and a medical doctor. Please send a stamped, self-addressed envelope with any enquiry.

EDUCATION AND SELF-HELP

Marylebone Health Centre
17 Marylebone Road
London NW1 5LT
Tel 01 935 6328

The centre has an educational unit which holds programmes and lectures on health and self-care. Please send a stamped, self-addressed envelope for further details.

FAMILY PLANNING AND FERTILITY

Family Planning Information Service
27-35 Mortimer Street
London W1N 7RJ
Tel 01 636 7866

The FPIS provides a nationwide enquiry service on all aspects of family planning, reproductive health and sexuality for both consumers and professionals. It has 11 regional centres around the UK. Information is available through a telephone enquiry service, leaflets and news sheets.

Foresight
Association for Preconceptual Care
The Old Vicarage
Church Lane
Witley
Godalming
Surrey, GU8 5PN

Foresight can give information on fertility related to nutrition, parental health, allergy and environment. They have a range of publications, and free leaflets. They can also provide the name of a local doctor in private practice who runs a Foresight clinic, and organize talks on preconceptual care to nurses, midwives, health visitors, and other interested groups. Please send a stamped, self-addressed envelope with any enquiries.

The National Association of Natural Family Planning Teachers
Birmingham Maternity Hospital
Queen Elizabeth Medical Centre
Edgbaston,
Birmingham B15 2TG
Tel 021 472 1377

This association helps to spread information on fertility. It reaches school teachers, parents, people involved in adult education programmes, and Family Life Programmes. They also publish books, periodicals, and organize lectures. The National Association of Natural Family Planning

Teachers is a registered charity. Please send a stamped, self-addressed envelope with all enquiries.

National Association for the Childless
Birmingham Settlement
318 Summer Lane
Birmingham B19 3RL
Tel 021 359 4887

This organization is a self-help support group offering advice and information to people experiencing infertility. They also offer help in dealing with your feelings towards various treatments, and how to cope if your treatment should fail. For more information please send a large stamped, self-addressed envelope.

GENERAL AND PSYCHOLOGICAL HELP

Arbours Association
6 Church Lane
London N8
Tel 01 348 7646

This association offers several services, which include a crisis centre, a training programme in psychotherapy, consultation services, and three long-stay households where individuals and couples can live in a supportive therapeutic environment. For more details on these services please send a stamped, self-addressed envelope with your enquiry.

MEDICAL AND HEALTH INFORMATION

Healthline
18 Victoria Square
London E2 9PF
Tel 01 980 4848

This organization provides a telephone service which gives detailed information on a wide range of medical and health problems including contraception. There are over 200 cassette tapes available which also include details on self-help groups relating to your problem. Some of these tapes offer information on symptoms, treatment, and how to seek proper medical advice. A special information service is available on AIDS. There is no charge for the information and all calls are charged as an ordinary phone call. Please send a stamped, self-addressed envelope with any enquiries.

PATIENT'S INTERESTS

Patient's Association
Room 33
18 Charing Cross Road
London WC2H 0HR
Tel 01 240 0671

This association promotes and protects the general interests of patients and gives advice on how to handle health problems. Information leaflets and a quarterly bulletin *Patients' Voice* are also available. *Self-Help and the Patient* is a directory of national organizations concerned with various diseases and handicaps, and the price will be given on request. Please send a stamped, self-addressed envelope with enquiries.

SMOKING

Action on Smoking and Health
5-11 Mortimer Street
London W1N 7RH
Tel 01 637 9843

This is a charitable organization which gathers information on the dangers of smoking. It also offers help on how to stop smoking. For further details send a stamped, self-addressed envelope.

WOMEN'S GENERAL HEALTH ISSUES

Brook Advisory Centres
153a East Street
London SE17 2SD
Tel 01 708 1234 *or* 01 708 1390

This association provides free and confidential advice for young people under 25 covering contraception, and aspects of maintaining a healthy reproductive system. Counselling is available for emotional and sexual problems. They can help with referral to special clinics, advice on AIDS, and provide speakers for youth orientated projects. For further details please send a stamped, addressed envelope with your enquiry.

Marie Stopes House
108 Whitfield Street
London W1P 6BE
Tel 01 388 0662 (2585)

This charitable organization offers a wide range of sexual health care services. Some of the areas covered are contraception, after-sex birth contol, pregnancy testing, gynaecological and menopausal problems, laboratory testing, complete physical exams, PMS, abortion counselling, and male and female sterilization. For further details please send a stamped, self-addressed envelope with any enquiry.

Women's Health Concern
Ground Floor
17 Earls Terrace
London W8 6LP
Tel 01 602 6669

This registered charity offers a specialist advisory service for menopause, PMS, and other female-related problems. Treatment, preventative health, and nutritional care are also available. They also publish a number of books on subjects relating to women's health. Please send a stamped, self-addressed envelope with all queries.

UNITED STATES

The Planned Parenthood Federation of America Inc
810 7th Avenue
N.Y., N.Y., 10019
Telephone 541-7800

International Women's Health Advisory Service
P.O. Box 31000
Phoenix, AZ 85046

National Women's Network
224 7th Street., S.E.,
Washington D.C. 20003

American Association of Naturopathic Physicians
P.O. Box 33046
Portland, OR 97233
Telephone 503/255-4863

American Holistic Medical Association
2727 Fairview Avenue, East.
No. G
Seattle. WA 98102

Consumer's Health and Medical Information Center
P.O. Box 390
Clearwater. FL 33517
Telephone 813/734-9016

International Foundation for Homeopathy
2366 Eastlake East
No. 301
Seattle. WA 98102
Telephone 206/324-8230

AUSTRALIA

The Family Planning Federation of Australia Inc
Suite 603
6th Floor
Roden Cutler House
24 Campbell Street
Sydney, NSW 2000
Telephone 211 1944

Chapter 10

THE FACT-FINDER

Adrenal gland Triangular-shaped gland next to each kidney which produces the corticosteroids, cortisone and adrenalin.

Allergy An abnormal reaction by body tissues to a specific substance which can occur after exposure to the same or similar substance to which the body has produced antibodies.

Amenorrhoea Menstrual periods which are absent even though there is no pregnancy or lactation.

Anaemia A reduction in the normal number of red blood cells. The body is unable to manufacture new cells fast enough to replace old cells.

   Anaemia, haemolytic Anaemia caused when the red blood cells are destroyed before their average life expectancy of 120 days in the bloodstream.

   Anaemia, megaloblastic Anaemia where abnormally large red blood cells containing a nucleus are found in the blood.

   Anaemia, pernicious Anaemia caused by vitamin B_{12} deficiency.

   Anaemia, sickle cell see **Sickle cell anaemia**

Antihypertensives Medicines used mainly to lower blood pressure by causing the walls of the blood vessels to expand. They may also inhibit the conversion of substances in the body which cause contraction of the blood vessels, thus relaxing the vessels and allowing the blood to flow more easily.

Anxiolytics Tranquillizers.

Arteriosclerosis Loss of elasticity in the artery walls due to thickening or hardening.

Artery Blood vessel carrying blood *away* from the heart.

Asthma Recurrent attacks of breathing difficulties caused by a decrease in the diameter of air passages. This decrease is the result of spasm of the bronchial tubes or swelling of their mucous membranes.

Atherosclerosis A form of arteriosclerosis which may be caused by the accumulation of fats, lipids, calcium deposits, carbohydrates, blood, and blood products on artery walls.

Benign A non-spreading, non-cancerous growth which is abnormal, and should not return after removal.

Bioavailability The extent and rate that metabolic substances, nutrients, or drugs enter general circulation.

Blood pressure, diastolic Blood pressure recorded when the heart muscle is relaxed and the heart is resting and refilling. This gives the lower reading when blood pressure is taken.

Blood pressure, systolic Blood pressure recorded when the heart muscle contracts and ejects blood, producing the maximum pressure in the larger arteries. This gives the higher reading when blood pressure is taken.

Blood sugar Formed during digestion, from starches, and absorbed from the intestines into the blood in the form of glucose, the simplest form of sugar.

Blood sugar disorders See **Hypoglycaemia, Hyperglycaemia,** and **Diabetes**

Break-through bleeding Abnormal spotting of blood in between menstrual periods or unexpected menstrual bleeding while taking the Pill.

Breast inflammation *See* **Mastitis**

Breast nodules *See* **Fibrocystic disease**

Bromelain An enzyme found in pineapple which digests protein. Like niacin, evening primrose oil, borage oil and blackcurrant-seed extract, it can stimulate the production of prostaglandin E_1.

Caffeine An alkaloid drug which dilates or opens up the blood vessels, stimulates the heart, increases the flow of urine, and may interfere with sleep. Caffeine can be found in the following: coffee, ordinary tea, chocolate, colas, matté and yerba sante tea, cocoa, some cold remedies and medicines, and guarana, which is one of the highest natural sources of caffeine.

Capillary An extremely narrow blood vessel, which connects the arteries and veins.

Carbohydrates Starches and sugars found mostly in vegetables, fruits and grains which provide most of the body's energy requirements.

Cardiovascular Referring to the heart and blood vessels.

Cataract Clouding of the lens of the eye resulting in blurred vision.

Cervical smear *See* **Pap smear**

Cervix Located at the bottom of the uterus, the cervix is the entrance to the womb, sometimes called the neck of the womb.

Chloasma Brown pigmentation of the face which may occur rarely during pregnancy or while using oral contraceptives.

Climacteric Referring to the menopause.

Clinical ecology A system of healing which focuses on the relationship between people and their environment, especially elements which cause health problems. A clinical ecologist will consider factors such as environmental chemicals, food preservatives, colouring and storage materials in order to make the patient aware of what may be causing individual health problems.

Contraception Prevention of conception.

Contraindication Any condition that makes a particular treatment or procedure undesirable. For example, a history of cardiovascular disease is a contraindication to taking oral contraceptives.

Corpus luteum A small yellow body which is formed in the ovary after the ovum has been discharged. It is known as an endocrine structure as it secretes the hormone progesterone. (For an explanation of its role in the menstrual cycle see chapter 2.)

D and C (Abbreviation for dilatation and curettage.) A minor operation whereby the cervix is expanded (dilatation) in order to insert an instrument which is used to scrape (curettage) the lining of the uterus. Often performed after miscarriage, induced abortion or when tissue samples are required for clinical tests.

Diabetes A metabolic disorder in which the body does not use carbohydrates efficiently. This can lead to a dangerously high level of glucose in the blood.

Diastolic pressure *See* **Blood pressure**

DNA The abbreviation for deoxyribonucleic acid, which is present in chromosomes found in the nuclei of cells. It is the chemical basis of heredity and carrier of genetic information.

Dubin-Johnson syndrome A disorder similar to jaundice which is due to an inherited defect in bile metabolism.

Dysmenorrhoea Painful menstrual periods.

Ectopic pregnancy A pregnancy which occurs outside the uterus in a fallopian tube or, more rarely, in the ovary or abdominal cavity. This type of pregnancy requires surgical intervention. Any pain occurring after a delayed, light, or missed period must be reported at once. The progestogen-only mini-Pill offers less protection against ectopic pregnancy than combined oral contraceptives.

Eczema Inflammation of the skin causing itching with a red rash, often accompanied by small weeping blisters.

Egg *See* **Ovum**

Embolism Obstruction of a blood vessel by a blood clot or foreign substance.

Embolus (From the Greek *embolus,* plug) A mass of undissolved matter present in a blood or lymph vessel, brought there by the blood or lymph flow.

Embryo The early stage of development of a foetus, from fertilization to about eight weeks.

Endocrine glands Ductless glands which secrete substances that are carried in the bloodstream or lymph and include the pituitary, thymus, pineal, thyroid, parathyroid, and adrenal glands, as well as the pancreas, ovaries, and testes.

Endometrium Mucous membrane lining the inner surface of the uterus which is prepared by hormones during the menstrual cycle to receive implantation of an embryo. It is shed as menstruation if no implantation occurs.

Epilepsy A disorder in which abnormal brain activity causes recurring changes in consciousness which can range from an attention lapse to loss of consciousness and convulsions.

Fallopian tube The tube or duct which conveys the ovum from the ovary to the uterus, and sperm towards the ovary.

Fertility The ability of the female to conceive, and for the male to produce sperm which are able to fertilize the female's egg.

Fibrin Protein, formed by the action of thrombin and fibrogen, which is the basis for blood clotting.

Fibrocystic breast disease The formation of nodules in the breast(s) accompanied by tenderness. Caused by an imbalance in the hormonal cycle associated with menstruation and fluctuates with the menstrual cycle.

Fibroids Muscle, and, rarely, fibrous tissue, which develops in lumps on the wall of the uterus. They usually cause no problems but may give rise to heavy or painful periods or discomfort in the pelvic region. Very rarely, they may interfere with fertility.

Foetus The name given to the unborn child after the third month of development.

Follicle A small sac in the ovary containing an ovum cell. At birth, the ovaries contain approximately half a million ova and these remain undeveloped until puberty when hormones stimulate their growth. A few follicles begin to develop at each menstrual cycle but usually only one completes the process and releases its ovum.

FSH The abbreviation for follicle stimulating hormone, which is produced by the pituitary gland. FSH stimulates the growth of follicles in the ovary, causing oestrogen production and the maturation of an egg cell. *See* **Follicle**

Gall stones Hard mass composed of bile pigments, cholesterol, and calcium salts which can form in the gall bladder.

Gamma linoleic acid (Also known as GLA) It is produced in the body by the conversion of linoleic acids and is one of the first steps in the production of prostaglandins which are important to many body functions. The conversion to GLA and the production of prostaglandins can be decreased or hindered by a diet high in saturated fats and processed foods, also by alcohol, stress, ageing and some disease conditions. Factors which help in the conversion are magnesium, zinc, selenium and vitamins B_6, B_3 and C. The use of evening primrose oil, blackcurrant seed and borage oils is a way of short-cutting the conversion process, as they already contain some GLA and a high percentage of cis-linoleic acid which is converted to prostaglandin E_1. (*See also* **Prostaglandins**.)

Genital herpes A sexually transmitted infection which is caused by the herpes simplex virus. It can produce single or multiple irritating blisters which affect the vagina, penis and surrounding skin. In women, it may also cause inflammation of the cervix with ulceration and a vaginal discharge.

Genital tract A term used for the reproductive system, which in the female consists of the uterus, cervix, vagina, right and left fallopian tubes and ovaries. In the male: testes, *vas deferens,* seminiferous tubules, seminal vesicles, urethra, and penis.

Guarana Prepared from the seeds of *Paullinia Cupana*, a tree of Brazil. It can be found in some slimming regimes or as a supplement and has a high caffeine content.

Gynaecologist A physician who specializes in female disorders of the reproductive system.

Gynaecology The study of diseases relating to women, especially of the reproductive system.

HCG (The abbreviation for human chorionic gonadotropin.) A hormone produced by cells of the placenta in the first months of pregnancy. HCG stimulates the secretion of oestrogen and progesterone by the corpus luteum.

HDL (The abbreviation for high density lipoprotein.) A useful blood fat which is thought to carry cholesterol through the bloodstream to where it can be harmlessly eliminated.

Hepatic Referring to the liver.

Herpes genitalis See **Genital herpes**

Hormone (From the Greek *hormon,* urging on.) A substance which is secreted from an organ or gland into the bloodstream. From there it is carried to another part of the body in order to stimulate or increase function, or to increase secretion of another hormone.

Hydatiform mole See **Trophoblastic disease**

Hydrogenated oils See **Hydrogenation**

Hydrogenation A process whereby oil is exposed to hydrogen, in the presence of a catalyst, to produce a solid fat. Margarines and hydrogenated and partially hydrogenated oils have been exposed to this process. Margarines and vegetable oils, theoretically high in polyunsaturated fats, become saturated when hydrogenated.

Hyperglycaemia High blood sugar, or an increase in blood sugar, as in **Diabetes**

Hypertension High blood pressure.

Hypnotics Also known as tranquillizers. Some belong to the drug group known as benzodiazepines which are addictive.

Hypoglycaemia Low blood sugar, or a deficiency of sugar in the blood.

Hypotension Low blood pressure.

Hypothalamus Part of the brain which is located above the pituitary gland and helps to control various body functions such as blood pressure, sleep, reproduction, water balance, emotional activity, body temperature, metabolism of fats and sugars, and appetite. It is of great importance in controlling the pituitary gland.

Immunity The body's system to protect it from substances it considers as 'foreign', which relies on the production of antibodies.

Infertility In the female, inability to conceive; in the male, inability to produce sperm capable of fertilizing an ovum.

IUD (The abbreviation for intra-uterine device.) A small device inserted into the uterus in order to prevent pregnancy by interfering with implantation of a fertilized egg or actually preventing fertilization.

Jaundice Increase in bile pigment in the blood, causing yellowing of the skin and eyes. Can be caused by disease of the liver, gall bladder, bile system or blood.

Lactation The production and secretion of milk by the mammary glands in the breasts. See also **Prolactin**

LH (The abbreviation for luteinizing hormone.) Produced by the pituitary gland, LH causes the release of an ovum and the production and maintenance of the **corpus luteum**

Libido The urge or drive usually associated with the sexual instinct.

Mammography A screening test for women who have breast lumps. X-rays are used to determine if the lumps are cancerous.

MAOIs The abbreviation for monoamine oxidase inhibitor drugs used for severe depression.

Mastitis Inflammation of the breast which may be due to hormonal or bacterial causes and can occur during lactation. Bacteria gain access to the breast through a crack in the nipple or via the mammary ducts.

Menopause The age at which menstruation ceases to occur.

Menorrhagia Heavy menstrual bleeding which is often prolonged.

Menstrual cycle The cycle of hormonal and other changes in a woman's body which leads to a discharge of blood from the uterus approximately every 28 days unless pregnancy occurs.

Metabolism The system of physical and chemical changes that take place within an organism to produce energy and assimilate new material for repair and replacement of tissues.

Migraine Recurring very severe headaches which may be caused by constriction of arteries to the head. Symptoms include severe pain, vision disturbances, nausea, vomiting and light sensitivity.

Monilia *See* **Thrush**

Myocardial infarction Heart attack.

Nephro Pertaining to the kidney.

NSAID (Abbreviation for non-steroidal anti-inflammatory drugs.) A group of drugs including aspirin and several other non-steroidal drugs used for pain, inflammation and fever.

Obstetrician A doctor who specializes in the care of pregnant women, and in the delivery of babies.

Oedema Swelling due to water retention, commonly in the fingers and ankles.

Oestriol A type of oestrogen hormone found in the urine of women.

Oestrogen Female sex hormones produced chiefly by the ovary, but also by the placenta during pregnancy.

Oligomenorrhoea Infrequent or scanty menstrual flow.

Osteoporosis Bone softening caused by a loss of minerals, especially calcium which is not replaced by normal reabsorption. This means that bones such as the spine and thigh become brittle and liable to fracture. Factors which can contribute to this condition are prolonged low dietary intake of calcium or other synergistic nutrients important for calcium metabolism, prolonged use of corticosteroid and some other drugs, prolonged immobility, menopausal hormonal changes, and increased urinary loss of calcium due to high protein diets.

Ovary The female sex gland in which ova cells are developed. The ovaries are the main producers of oestrogen.

Ovulation The release of the ovum from the ovary.

Ovum The female reproductive cell, also known as an egg. It is 1/10 of a millimetre in diameter and, although microscopically small, is the largest cell in the body.

Pap smear A test devised by Dr Papanicolaou. It involves the removal of cells from the surface of the cervix by gently scraping with a sterile spatula. The cells are then sent for laboratory examination to determine whether they are cancerous. This test is useful for early detection of cancer and may also be used for detection of non-malignant tissue changes.

Phlebitis Inflammation, pain and tenderness in a vein.

PID (The abbreviation for pelvic inflammatory disease.) This is caused by an infection and inflammation of the ovaries, fallopian tubes, and surrounding tissues. Some of the symptoms are pain or discomfort during sexual intercourse, increased vaginal discharge accompanied by an odour, and pains in the lower abdomen. Because progestogens thicken cervical mucus it may be more difficult for bacteria to penetrate the cervix and reach the reproductive organs, so the Pill may decrease the chance of developing PID.

Pituitary gland A small gland at the base of the brain which produces hormones including follicle-stimulating hormone and luteinizing hormone. It is also sometimes referred to as the 'master gland' of the body because it releases hormones which can affect body growth, reproduction and other bodily processes.

Placenta (More commonly called the 'after-birth'.) An oval-shaped organ which is responsible for nourishing the foetus or baby while still in its womb. The placenta manufactures the hormones in the mother which are responsible for changes in her body during pregnancy. This organ is discharged from the body after the baby is born.

Platelet Disc-shaped element of the blood, necessary for clotting.

Polymenorrhoea Menstrual periods which occur regularly, but too frequently.

Porphyria A very rare disorder of the metabolism, usually congenital, in which porphyrins, purple products of haemoglobin decomposition, accumulate abnormally in tissues and are excreted in increased amounts in the urine and faeces. Symptoms include mild to severe pigmentation of the skin, sensitivity to sunlight, discoloration of teeth and bones, neurological, muscle and psychological disorders.

Progesterone A steroid sex hormone produced by the corpus luteum, adrenal glands or placenta. It prepares the uterus for pregnancy during the second half of the menstrual cycle and is responsible for important developments in the placenta and breasts during pregnancy. This hormone has effects all over the body, including the slight rise in body temperature during the second half of the menstrual cycle, which is the basis of the temperature method of family planning.

Progestogen A naturally produced or synthetic hormone which produces effects similar to those of progesterone. It may be administered orally or by injection.

Prolactin A hormone produced by the pituitary gland which, in conjunction with oestrogen and progesterone, stimulates breast development and the formation of milk during pregnancy.

Prophylaxis Prevention.

Prostaglandins Hormone-like substances derived from fatty acids which help to stimulate the movement of smooth muscle in the body. Prostaglandins affect the heart rate and blood pressure and can encourage the uterine contractions. Prostaglandin E_1 is anti-inflammatory and can have a beneficial effect on the cardiovascular and reproductive systems.

Renal Referring to the kidney.

RH (The abbreviation of releasing hormone.) Several RHs are secreted by the hypothalamus, located underneath the thalamus in the brain. Releasing hormones control the release of various hormones including those of the pituitary gland.

Salpingitis See **PID**

Semen A thick secretion containing sperm, which is discharged during the male orgasm.

Sickle cell anaemia An abnormality of haemoglobin where some red blood cells become crescent shaped which can interfere with normal oxygen transport because the red blood cells cannot pass through the very fine capillaries in the body's main organs and in the extremities. It occurs mainly in people of African or Mediterranean descent.

Spermicide A substance which can kill sperm. It is used for contraception with other methods such as the condom or cap.

Sterilization An operation which can be performed on either sex to prevent pregnancy. It is usually difficult or impossible to reverse. Sterilization usually involves only the blocking of uterine tubes in the female or the *vas deferens* in the male, but, in some cases, usually because of disease, the uterus, ovaries or testicles may be removed.

Stroke Usually sudden paralysis as a result of an interruption in the flow of blood to the brain by a clot or by rupture of an artery wall.

Symptomatic relief Short-term relief of symptoms.

Synergistic Working together to produce a better effect.

Systemic Pertaining to the whole body.

Systolic pressure *See* **Blood pressure**

Thromboembolism The blocking of a blood vessel by a thrombus that has become detached from its site of formation.

Thrombophlebitis The inflammation of a vein caused by a blood clot in it.

Thrombosis The formation, development or existence of a blood clot in a blood vessel.

Thrombus A blood clot which obstructs a blood vessel or cavity.

Thrush A yeast infection caused by *candida albicans*. Some areas affected can be the mouth, throat and vagina.

Triglycerides Fats and lipids produced in the liver from carbohydrates. In excess, in the blood stream, they can contribute to atherosclerosis.

Trophoblastic disease A type of tumour or growth in the placenta which may rarely develop in pregnancy. It prevents the fertilized egg from further development. If the tumour is benign it is often referred to as a 'hydatiform mole'.

Urethra A tube through which urine and semen are passed.

Urinary tract Organs and ducts which secrete and eliminate urine. The urinary system consists of the kidneys, ureters, urinary bladder and urethra.

Uterine tubes *See* **Fallopian tubes**

Uterus A muscular organ, also known as the womb. It is a pear-shaped hollow in which the foetus grows during pregnancy. (*See also* **Endometrium**)

Varicose veins Enlarged, twisted veins which commonly occur in the legs but may appear in almost any part of the body.

Vascular Referring to the blood vessels.

Vas deferens The tube which carries sperm from the testes to the urethra.

Vulva External female genitalia which surround the vagina.

Womb See **Uterus**

BIBLIOGRAPHY

ABPI Data Sheet Compendium 1988-89, Datapharm Publications Ltd.
British National Formulary (Number 14), The Pharmaceutical Press, 1987.
Contraception: Your questions answered, John Guillebaud, Churchill Livingston, 1986.
Dorland's Illustrated Medical Dictionary (24th Edition), Saunders, 1965.
Drug-induced Nutritional Deficiencies (2nd Edition), Daphne A. Roe, AVI Publishing Co., Westport, Connecticut, 1978.
Drug/nutrient Interrelationships: Nutrition and pharmacology: An interphase of disciplines, Nutrition Society of Canada, McMaster University, Hamilton, 1974.
Drugs and Nutrients, Vol. 21: The interactive effects, Daphne A. Roe and T. Colin Campbell (eds.), Marcel Dekker Inc., 1984.
Essential Human Anatomy and Physiology, Barbara R. Landau, Scott, Foreman and Company, 1976.
Human Fertility Control: Theory and practice, Hawkins & Elder, Butterworths, 1979.
Martindale's The extra pharmacopoeia (28th Edition), The Pharmaceutical Press, 1982.
Review of Medical Physiology (10th Edition), William F. Ganong MD, Lange Medical Publications, 1981.
The Medicine Chest, Gillian Martlew ND and Shelley Silver, Thorsons, 1988.
Mental and Elemental Nutrients, Carl Pfeiffer PhD, MD, Keats, 1975.
Taber's Cyclopedic Medical Dictionary (15th Edition), Clayton L. Thomas MD MPH (ed.) F. A. Davis Company, 1985.
Textbook of Contraceptive Practice, John Peel and Malcolm Potts, Cambridge University Press, 1983.

Magazines, medical journals and publications

Adverse Drug Reaction Bulletin
American Journal of Clinical Nutrition
American Journal of Obstetrics and Gynecology
British Journal of Family Planning
British Journal of Sexual Medicine
British Medical Journal
Modern Medicine
New Scientist
Quarterly Journal of Medicine
Update

INDEX